The Power of Belonging

The Power of Belonging

How to Develop Safety, Inclusion, and Belonging for Leaders and Organizations

Sunita Sehmi

BEP
BUSINESS EXPERT PRESS
Leader in applied, concise business books

First published in 2021 by
Business Expert Press, LLC
222 East 46th Street, New York, NY 10017
www.businessexpertpress.com

ISBN-13: 978-1-95334-986-6 (paperback)
ISBN-13: 978-1-95334-987-3 (e-book)

Business Expert Press Business Career Development Collection

Collection ISSN: 2642-2123 (print)
Collection ISSN: 2642-2131 (electronic)

First edition: 2021

10 9 8 7 6 5 4 3 2 1

To my favorite Arjun
et à mon préféré Kabir

Description

This book is for anyone who wants to achieve better personal and organizational effectiveness and fruitful business relationships. It is designed to give both the theoretical knowledge and the tools for action to change your organization's power dynamics. To operate in a global environment that is increasingly relational than transactional, it is vital to cultivate globally competitive leaders to deal with ongoing change and challenges. *The Power of Belonging* addresses these challenges faced by leaders today, both when influencing and achieving organizational goals.

This is also a book for individuals too, because we cannot define ourselves by single dimensions—we are a synthesis of our backgrounds, experiences and philosophies. Thus, the most challenging lesson to learn is that belonging will remain a puzzle until we find that it has a unique dwelling place—that we must first profoundly belong to ourselves. So are you ready to be a change agent? Great then this book is for you!

Keywords

the power of belonging; leadership; organizations; motivation; performance; profit; retention; wellbeing

Contents

Foreword

My feeling of never genuinely belonging—not in my family of origin, not in my community, nor my country of birth—left me with a lack of psychological safety. Consequently, I spent most of my life trying to *fit in*, as I was so eager to be part of something, a group, a collective … somehow and in some way.

I have lived, breathed, and suffered at times, due to exclusion and not belonging, and I know that I am not alone. My experiences gave birth to my purpose, my drive, and indeed to this book.

My parents were immigrants from Punjab who left India in the mid-1950s for Britain, seeking better opportunities for themselves and their families. Less than a decade before, they had endured the trauma of the India–Pakistan partition.

As a child of immigrants, I spent much time as an external spectator of two value systems, British and Indian, without ever participating fully and with a feeling of belonging to neither. I spent most of my life on the outside looking in, trying to belong somewhere, trying to understand the *in* group whilst being in the minority, the *out* group. I had a constant internal longing to be an insider, yet knew I did not fully fit in. I realized that I had two lives in parallel—a relationship with the home country and one with the host country.

India, for me, remained mysterious and enigmatic, and I crafted a story about my parents' homeland from the snippets and mixture of all that I had heard second hand. When I was growing up, part of me wanted to shed my Indian heritage. I felt like the outsider. But now, I appreciate just how magnificent my ancestry is, and I am privileged to represent my family's country of origin.

Indeed, as I have seen in the research, belonging is an emotional state, which can have far-reaching consequences on achievement and health. The longing for belonging can be so omnipresent that it impacts everything we do.

My background has left me with a strong sense of being a connector. In the work that I do, I realize that we need to acknowledge that we all have very similar needs, concerns, and hopes. How we connect on these similarities is central to all human relationships. This realization has become a passion that is the driver of my purpose, personally and professionally.

My hope with this book is to give you an opportunity to explore and to understand the concept of belonging in organizations and why it has become so important in organizational life. How come we are talking about inventory and inclusion, belonging and budgets, all in the same breath? Have we always wanted to belong at work? Or, has this become a need to cope with modern working life? So, this book, from a historical concept, is a psychological and anthropological view of belonging and how to implement belonging at work and beyond. How this impacts us all on a human as well as an organizational level. I have dedicated a large segment of this book to a series of interviews that I undertook with 129 people. I asked six open-ended questions on the topic of belonging. Once I had collated all results, I used the grounded theory to discover emerging patterns in data. Indeed, I saw several themes that emerged from these interviews.

I found this exercise extremely interesting and also profoundly insightful. These were thoughts and feelings from real people and what they felt about organizational belonging, and indeed, what it means not to belong.

I hope you enjoy reading this book, and as always, that it leaves you curious and with more questions on this topic.

Dear reader
In this book, my wish is that you walk away knowing the following:

- *How to create a resilient, future-proof organizational culture where people belong and feel safe to be themselves.*
- *How to create an ethos that values respect and acceptance.*
- *How to create a culture of organizational belonging.*
- *How to truly create greater inclusivity for you, your team, and your organization.*

The aims of this book are:

- *To highlight the importance of studying the concept of belonging.*
- *To clarify and define "belonging," inclusion and authenticity.*
- *To offer a theoretical overview of different aspects of belonging.*
- *To provide frameworks for exploring belonging.*
- *To introduce an appreciation of different ideas about belonging and organizations.*

Preface

Longing for Belonging

Here is my secret; it is only with the heart that one can see rightly.
What is essential is invisible to the eye
> —Antoine de Saint-Exupéry from The Little Prince.

Each one of us can remember a moment when we felt we did not belong. It is not a feeling one can forget. The unique power of belonging and the detrimental effects of not belonging play out every day in our society. Indeed, there is a difference between feeling included and belonging. Inclusion is about the here and now. Belonging is about the past and possible future. And, the feeling of belonging continues even when we are not physically together.

In all the work I have done on diversity and inclusion (known as D&I), I have found that simply being included does not mean you belong.

Unless people in an organization genuinely feel they belong, regardless of how diverse they might be, their full potential may never be recognized—no matter how hard an organization has worked on their D&I strategy, nothing drives the message home more than belonging.

Belonging is a feeling and a far more powerful force than any D&I strategy could ever be. It is a fundamental human need that translates across any language or culture and a feeling that every human is wired to strive for. Pat Wadors, who is credited with creating the term DIB (diversity, inclusion, and belonging) beautifully states: "D&I may capture your head but belonging captures your heart."

I remain curious about how some organizations, communities, and families connect with people. How are they able to provide unreserved approval, instinctively knowing what is going on for people? How do they have a sense that another may be struggling? And know that some of us are not comfortable to share our real fears, especially at the risk of feeling judged?

The significance of belonging and inclusion has become increasingly acute as the world deals with massive demographic, cultural, environmental, and technological transformation. What I know for sure is that the speed at which organizations are changing is overwhelming and, for some of us, challenging. The only thing we can be certain of today is that change is a sure thing, and our inability to adapt to everchanging contexts and diverse people will lead to disappointment and perhaps even ruin a career.

There is a need for a new workforce to deal with this constant change—and this is a workforce that can understand people wherever they are from and their needs, and particularly people in the global context. Never before has the power of belonging and inclusion been so essential for the sustainability of an organization.

Indeed, the link between belonging and inclusion and organizational success is recognized. Over the last 10 years, the words *belonging*, and *inclusion* have become central to our professional and personal communities.

Research Study

The choice for my research subject arose from my experience in the field of D&I. It was also driven by my Indian-British-Swiss background. The disharmony between philosophies left me wandering and despondent about the principle of belonging; the feeling of safety and care; the appreciation for the uniqueness of each member of a specific group or place. The literature available on belonging resonated with me.

I have met and worked with drivers and leaders of change, and the primary purpose of my research project was to explore, investigate, and understand their experiences of belonging and the impact it has had and continues to have on them.

This research process was incredibly stimulating, as it was my first solo attempt at research after so many years. Indeed in 1985, my bachelor thesis asked the question, "How do minority groups perceive 'other' minority groups in Britain?" I was surprised by how much I learned about being reflective and about appreciating how my own process of learning and looking for truth would impact the study.

Arising out of this research, I based my interviews around the definition attributed to the late Carl Rogers, founder of the humanistic psychology movement and father of client-centered therapy. He defines belonging as, "An exclusive and individual experience that relates to a longing for connection with others, the requisite for positive regard and the yearning for interpersonal connection."

You will notice that at the end of each chapter is a section from my research. It is filled with book quotes from participants expressing how they felt about belonging and not belonging in their professional lives. These were thoughts and feelings from real people and what they felt about organizational belonging, and indeed, what it means not to belong.

I have used my research as a base for this book. I ran a series of interviews where I asked six open-ended questions on the topic of belonging. I interviewed 129 people, 71 men, and 58 women. Participants were professionals from more than 40 countries and from 25 activity sectors. I interviewed 105 participants before the Covid-19 crisis and then another 24 at the beginning of the pandemic. People and company names have been anonymized.

What become apparent for me throughout the research and the discussions with clients is that there are feelings of frustration toward senior management.

When top management assert that they want to create a sense of belonging and do not walk the talk, this causes resentment. Employees are looking for meaning in their work and an authentic culture where everyone is responsible, accountable, and conscientious. They also understand that a *one-size-fits-all* approach will not work; differences must be seen and acknowledged. At the same time, I clearly saw how belonging was everyone's responsibility It is crucial for psychological safety[1].

I found during my D&I interventions in many organizations and countries that, no matter our experience, skin color, gender, or sexual orientation, we all want to belong. This is why, organizational belonging transcends D&I; it is about everyone.

---

[1] Psychological safety is being able to show and employ one's self without fear of negative consequences of self-image, status, or career (Kahn 1990; p. 708). It can be defined as a shared belief that the team is safe for interpersonal risk-taking.

However, it was also during my D&I workshops that I witnessed a lack of understanding and consideration of the importance of belonging in organizations. In late 2019 and early 2020, I undertook a research study to explore and understand how belonging is perceived in organizations and in life. The results of this research have been used to underpin and illustrate some of the ideas in this book.

The most difficult lesson to learn perhaps, is that belonging will remain a puzzle until we find that it has a personal dwelling place—that we must first belong deeply to ourselves.

And, of course, it is a book for myself, as I looked to satisfy my curiosity about what is really happening in organizations in their attempts to create a sense of belonging for their employees. Having worked with and across different contexts for over 25 years, I had noticed a shift in the way that I myself worked. I found myself focusing on giving people the tools to connect with others, to build relationships, and to look beyond the culture that can sometimes blind us. I wondered whether others were doing the same.

We are living in thought-provoking times, where we must revolutionize and examine how to futureproof our organizations to become levers of change. My wish is that this book will help you drive real change in your organization.

In summary, these themes constituted the findings from the research:

Defining a Sense of Belonging

Belonging is related to the human need to establish connections with other people. Participants in the survey understood the sense of belonging to mean being part of social groups or organizations where there are shared interests and beliefs, and where there is an emotional component that derives from feeling included, accepted, and recognized. Achieving a sense of belonging in organizations has some particular connotations, including good relationships with co-workers, interest in personal circumstances outside of work, and recognition for roles and contributions. There is a need for an environment where all employees feel the confidence to express themselves freely, and where inclusion and acceptance are promoted.

Belonging in the Workplace

Individuals, especially younger generation, need to identify with the organization's values and mission. When this does not happen, there is a high chance of them looking for other job alternatives. There is also risk of ill health. Conversely, high identification leads to happiness, positive impact on health, and job satisfaction. The more employees can identify with the values of their organization and become involved with its mission and goals, the more they experience a sense of belonging. The challenge for organizations is to create a collective awareness around a common purpose and to recognize the contribution of each member of the team.

Benefits of Belonging for Employees and Organizations

A sense of belonging has benefits for both employees and organizations. When individuals feel that they are listened to, respected, accepted, and that their contribution is valued, this generates happiness, increases their motivation and commitment to the organization, productivity and loyalty increase, and they will want to stay longer.

The Impact of a Sense of Nonbelonging

When individuals feel that they do not fit into a group or organization, and feel ignored, alone, excluded, and rejected, they can experience the same sensations as physical pain. The effects can be a deterioration in physical and mental health, poor self-esteem, decreased motivation and productivity, increased absenteeism, and poor retention of talent. All of this will result in an economic cost to the organization. Unhappiness can also spill over into the home.

The Management of Not Belonging

Different individuals manage the lack of sense of belonging in different ways. Some look for alternative employment; some turn to friends, family, or therapists; others turn to alcohol. More proactive and resilient methods involve thinking differently about the relationship between an organization and its employees. When individuals stop depending on organizations to provide meaning in their lives, it opens the way for better self-awareness and the acceptance of personal responsibility for relationships and opportunities.

Challenges for Organizations

Organizations are faced with a diversity of ideas, experiences, and cultures; the demands of new generations; remote work; and the need for new management approaches based on the emotions of individuals. This is a challenge requiring profound transformations. Effort is required by everyone—the organization itself, leaders and managers, and every employee—to ensure that everyone feels included and accepted; that employees who are miles away are involved in the mission of the organization, and that new talents are retained.

Strategies to Develop a Sense of Belonging in Organizations

Participants listed some specific actions that organizations could take to develop a sense of belonging in the organization. These included listening to employees' concerns, involving them in decision making, creating spaces for them to interact and to bond, and defining roles and responsibilities so that they know how they are contributing to the goals of the organization.

Acknowledgments

I would like to sincerely thank all the people who so kindly participated in my research.

They offered their precious time and shared information generously and openly. I am forever indebted to them and truly thankful for their patience and trust. And, I would like to thank all those people who never felt they truly belonged. Watching the insiders from the outside and longing to belong, but never really feeling part of the collective.

To my tribe, I thank you from the bottom of my heart. This is for you.

My tribe don't all look like me,
My tribe is composed of people from different backgrounds and ethnicity.
My tribe doesn't think the same, it challenges, it pushes, it doesn't
play the game.
My tribe has no fear to call it out, to say when it's not ok, to shout it out.
My tribe is unique, not a clique, it's proud to be distinct,
My tribe is free.

CHAPTER 1

Belonging in Organizations

To be kept in solitude is to be kept in pain and put on the road to madness. A person's membership in his group—his tribe—is a large part of his identity.

—E. O. Wilson

People are a vital component of the performance of any organization and developing a workforce that is committed and loyal requires perpetual investment. A sense of belonging is an essential trait for competitive corporations because of its impact on performance. At the same time, it contributes to the emotional welfare of employees because it meets their fundamental need for connection[1].

What energizes effectiveness in any organization is, first and foremost, a sense of inclusion and belonging and only then operational activities. In a healthy work climate, people have fun at work, perform their tasks with enthusiasm, and are happy to come to work in the morning.

Defining Organizational Culture

Peter Drucker famously said, "Culture eats strategy for breakfast." You might have the best strategy in the world, but if your culture does not support it, there are costs. Organizational culture can be defined as a set of knowledge, practices, norms, and beliefs that make up the social and psychological environment of a group or business. It includes values, rules, and rituals that shape the attitudes and behaviors of the members of the group. The practices of individuals are, therefore, not spontaneous; they are "standardized" and conditioned by the culture. The values that make

---

[1] Proof that positive work cultures are more productive HBR by Emma Seppälä and Kim Cameron, December 01, 2015.

up this culture are ideals and moral principles that give broad guidelines to the group's actions.

Culture drives many aspects of organizational life, including decision making, rewards, promotions, how people are treated, and so on. It influences people's attitudes and behaviors at work and has a strong impact on performance. It defines how people act in difficult situations; how they handle pressure and challenges; how they treat customers, colleagues, and each other.

One of the ways to support belonging is to have an organizational culture that facilitates belonging. Another is to ensure that there is the sense of alignment between personal and organizational values.

Organizational culture is not static. It is particularly sensitive to the moods of the people who define it. It is created most strongly by the actions of the leaders of the organization—as always, actions speak louder than words here. It is not enough to simply have a transcribed vision and list of values. The goal is to generate an environment where people are engaged, passionate, and prepared to execute your strategy.

And, in today's global world, one of the primary talents of leaders is the ability to manage change and leverage difference. They are required to deal with challenges, friction, and misunderstandings stemming from diversity, physical distance, and technology. This is where belonging fits in.

How can you as a leader make sure that you have created an environment and a set of values, norms, and practices that allow people from a variety of backgrounds to feel comfortable, recognized, and valued? Belonging inspires your team to feel safe and creates optimal conditions for health and well-being—and then for productivity. Without this, achieving your strategy can be very problematic.

Experiencing Belonging in Organizations

I found, when speaking to participants during the interview phase of my research, that a sense of belonging is developed by sharing the company's philosophy, mission, and vision, and by advocating adherence to corporate values. Very often, it includes a strong awareness of organizational history. However, there needs to be a link between theory and practice, with espoused values being put into practice by the management team.

The EY 2019 Belonging Barometer[2] undertook research with more than 1,000 employed American adults. The results showed that when people felt like they belonged, they were more productive, motivated, and engaged. It was reported that a strong sense of belonging leads to better collaboration, retention, and business performance. Besides this, it significantly reduces stress levels and improves physical health, emotional well-being, and performance.

Another important finding was that employees had an expectation for both belonging and diversity in the workplace. In fact, nearly half believed that diversity is best represented at work, and more than a third said that it was in the workplace that they most experienced a sense of belonging. They experienced a lesser sense of belonging in their neighborhoods and even in their places of worship.

Participants in the EY study (particularly baby boomers and Gen Xers) believed that a sense of belonging was engendered by being both trusted and respected. Likewise, by being able to speak freely and voice their opinions and by having their unique contributions recognized. When there was not a sense of belonging, the overwhelming emotion described was that of being ignored. Furthermore, according to another study, men tended also to feel stressed, while women reported feeling sad. It was also reported that millennials experienced loneliness as a result of not belonging, reporting that exclusion was a form of bullying.

My own research reflected a similar theme, where participants admitted that when inclusion, acceptance, and recognition were in alignment with the values of the organization, this was seen as essential to developing a sense of belonging in an organization. Besides this, an important aspect was the need for organizations to recognize their *human* side, with a management style focused on the emotions of individuals. It is not enough to talk about belonging—it must be promoted, and there must be real transformation. *Human management* in the workplace is an essential criterion.

According to participants, organizations should understand the shift in relationships from a balance of power to collaboration and

---

[2] EY Belonging Barometer study *May 11, 2019.*

communication. Employees want to have friends at work; connect with the organization's mission and values; be included, accepted, and recognized; they want to be happy and healthy; and, above all, they want the work that they do to be meaningful. Excessive work hours are now not acceptable; they want to have free time to share with family and friends.

However, some participants also emphasized that the responsibility for developing a sense of belonging should not rest exclusively with the human resources office but also with managers and employees, affirming that everyone can work together to promote a safe, belonging, and inclusive work environment.

Nevertheless, an organization cannot be expected to create a sense of belonging if employees themselves are not willing to cooperate. Employees must strive to develop ties with co-workers, to show respect and affection. As one participant emphasized, you cannot belong if *you* do not make the effort to engage with others.

The role of leaders was also highlighted by participants. Employees are looking to their people managers to promote a happy work environment, where they feel safe to share their ideas, where they feel free to be themselves.

The feeling of belonging is the identification and specific attachment to a reference group adhering to shared values and characteristics. All the members of a social group must be aware of belonging to this group and must interact more or less directly with each other. This distinguishes a social group from a simple grouping of individuals.

Similarly, a team represents a group of people working collectively toward a common goal. It necessitates cohesion, communication, and collaboration, and importantly, it requires personal effort from all team members to make it work. Being in a team where there is a high trust and high psychological safety does not only translate into a high sense of belonging, it also renders into team effectiveness. While we know this to be true instinctively, it has been confirmed by research.

In 1999, Amy Edmondson, professor at Harvard Business School, identified psychological safety as a key factor for effective teams. This was described by her as:

A sense of confidence that the team will not embarrass, reject or punish someone for speaking up. It describes a team climate characterized by interpersonal trust and mutual respect in which people are comfortable being themselves.

This is not to be mistaken for being nice, she says. It is about giving candid feedback, openly admitting mistakes, asking for help, and learning from each other.

Psychological Study Project Aristotle by Google

The need for psychological safety was confirmed in a three-year-long study undertaken by Google, titled Project Aristotle. This name was to reflect the philosopher's quotation that "the whole is greater than the sum of its parts."

Google sought to build the perfect team, and the research team in 2011 set about studying hundreds of teams in Google's 114,000 employees to find what made for the best results. They realized that there were certain group norms that defined teams, but despite the massive amount of data that they had, they could not find a consistent pattern of what made some teams more successful than others. Until they stumbled on the theory of psychological safety. They were then able to use their data to demonstrate that, regardless of the make-up or purpose of the team, the one consistent requirement for success was that people were equally heard, and that they had a degree of empathy for each other.

As Charles Duhigg[3] wrote in the *New York Times*:

The paradox, of course, is that Google's intense data collection and number-crunching have led it to the same conclusions that good managers have always known. In the best teams, members listen to one another and show sensitivity to feelings and needs.

Amy Edmundson agrees, stating in her book *Fearless Organizations*[4], this sense of security and trust is essential for employee retention, as

---

[3] What Google Learned From Its Quest to Build the Perfect Team New research reveals surprising truths about why some work groups thrive and others falter. By Charles Duhigg, NY Times Magazine February 25, 2016.

[4] Amy Edmundson Fearless Organizations.

psychological safety is a fundamental part of the employment contract. When this is not the case, research suggests that it leads inexorably to higher turnover and absenteeism rates, lower productivity, and other harmful outcomes.

We all know when we are in a *psychologically safe* team, because it allows us to have critical conversations; it enables us to dare, meaning to challenge authority, give feedback in *real time*, build trust, and grow together. It can move successfully from a transactional to a relational model of communication. As Edmundson states in her book *"Speaking up is only the first step… and then the true test is how leaders respond when people actually do speak up."*

When the team is not psychologically safe, it can have a devastating impact on its members. Indeed an interesting observation from my research exposed how participants felt in response to their own not-belonging either manifesting as emotional paralysis or *brain freeze.* Certainly, research shows that the *fight or flight* reaction effectively disables the executive function of the brain, leaving us with the raw emotions and less logical rationale.

From a Transactional to Relational Business Agenda

Our global business world is becoming increasingly relational versus transactional, so genuine connection means we have to focus on the whole person, the entire person, the person who shows up, and not the person we *think* they are. When we are part of an organization, a team, or a family where we are safe and included, this gives the feeling that our genuine self is applauded and admired. There is no *persona* as Carl Jung described, no guise, no pretext; rather, there is a feeling that we can take our masks off, be ourselves, and feel comfortable contributing. In teams where there is healthy belonging, people are allowed to be themselves, to meet themselves, and have a strong sense of being seen and heard. When people cannot be themselves, many will try to fit in by assimilating to the dominant culture. This phenomenon is known as covering or masking.

A Deloitte study of more than 3,000 people found that 61 percent of the people cover at work on at least one dimension. This is more prevalent if they are black (79 percent) or gay (83 percent). An interesting finding of this study was that over 40 percent of straight white males (often regarded as the dominant culture) said that they also masked at work. Clearly, the issues of inclusion apply to everyone. And, up to 73 percent of the people surveyed said that masking or covering was detrimental to their sense of self, and half said that it reduced their commitment to the organization.

Benefits of belonging for employees and organizations

A sense of belonging has benefits for both employees and organizations. When individuals feel that they are listened to, respected, accepted, and that their contribution is valued, this generates happiness, increases their motivation and commitment to the organization, productivity, and loyalty increase, and they will want to stay longer.

Being able to be ourselves is not about vulnerability—it is about non-defensiveness. It is about not having to manage your identity along with managing your job, as one participant in the Deloitte study put it. It allows us to be with our feelings. We can be with ourselves and then be with others. Organizations and teams that provide a supportive environment and caring behavior create a sense of trust and safety.

Indeed, an alignment of values is beneficial to both the employee and the organization. Participants believed that employees' commitment to the organization's mission will be higher, there will be more loyalty, and they will want to stay longer.

Identification with the organization's mission and values seems to have the same effect on team members as having strong and stable social relationships with others. It is a source of happiness and has a positive impact on health. It is a key indicator for job satisfaction.

To develop a sense of belonging, people must be able to identify with the team, the organization, or the brand for which they work. Group membership is a mixture of a sense of usefulness to a group and solidarity with a team and is a powerful indicator of the spirit of belonging. It makes it easier for the employee to adapt the company's values, codes, and ethics. They will find meaning in their activities and will be more efficient.

The Power of Belonging

Power of Belonging: Reflective-Exercise

1. What are your thoughts, beliefs, and values about belonging in your organizational context?
2. How do your thoughts about belonging relate to your workplace relationships?
3. What alignments or misalignments *vis-à-vis* belonging do you notice within the organizational context?
4. Can you begin to reflect on the possibilities and the benefits of belonging within your organization?

Findings and Quotes From My Research

Alignment With the Values of the Organization

The affiliation between the values of the organization and the values of employees is an essential element in the development of the sense of belonging in organizations. Participants expressed their desire to fit into the culture of their workplace, and this included identification with the organization's values, mission, and goals.

> *I am proud to work for my organization because I am part of a clear and concrete project and ambition. I am part of a group of individuals who share the same corporate values.*
>
> —Director of Operations, Telecom

When the work they do does not correspond to their own values, the disconnection with the organization can lead employees to look for other job alternatives. It can also negatively impact their health. Conversely, when they identify with the values of their organization and become involved in its mission and goals, their sense of belonging increases. This alignment contributes more to a sense of belonging than remuneration and conditions of employment.

*Doing this interview has already made me aware how unsafe I felt...
I couldn't trust anyone... I was scared to talk about the real issues
with the powers above me because I saw people who did got rejected
and ejected in some way. I didn't fit in and my health was actually
impacted because I didn't feel safe and I did not belong, so I left.*
—Director, Oil and Gas Industry

*How can we feel proud to belong to an entity if we find no meaning
in it, if the direction is not clear?*
—Head of Facilities, Transport Industry

*Compensation or working conditions have no impact on the sense of
belonging. A volunteer may feel a strong sense of belonging to a group
because he or she feels recognized and shares its values.*
—Head of Supply Chain, Manufacturing

Participants saw that leaders had a critical role in involving employees with the organizational values.

*Employees look to managers to know the rules, to understand the
company's culture and how it operates. It is up to them to promote
inclusive behavior among employees.*
—Strategy Consultant, Consulting Industry

Some participants in management positions discussed their efforts to develop a sense of belonging through ensuring that employees knew the value of the work they performed and their contribution to the organization's mission.

*We have a very clear corporate mission that gives employees the feeling
that they are contributing to something important to their company.
This values their efforts and motivates them to move towards something they believe in.*
—HRBP, Wine and Spirits

CHAPTER 2

History of Belonging

You only are free when you realize you belong no place—you belong every place—no place at all.

—Maya Angelou

Defining Belonging

Very early definitions of the word *belong (v.)* go back to the mid-14th century Middle English, where it was defined as "to go along with, properly relate to," and from the Old English langian "pertain to, to go along with." Meanings of "be the property of" and "be a member of" were first recorded in the late 14th century.

It is similar to the Middle Dutch *belanghen*, the Dutch *belangen*, and the German *belangen*.

The Cambridge Dictionary defines belonging as feeling happy or comfortable in a situation. It also refers to the feeling a person has of being in the right place.

Dictionary.com defines the noun *belonging* or *belongingness* as a secure relationship; affinity.

A list of synonyms and antonyms also gives us a sense of what belonging is about: closeness, familiarity, inseparability, nearness—and its opposite: distance.

Evolution stipulates that we are social animals, innately predetermined to construct relationships and communities to survive and thrive. The history of our oldest ancestors demonstrates how belonging was necessary for survival. From the moment we are born, we try to connect with our primary caregivers—this is part of attachment theory. In the times of hunters and gatherers, belonging to a group was a question of survival, as being alone could result in physical harm or death.

Consequently, not belonging fires up the same neurons in our brain as hunger and thirst[1].

There are hundreds of definitions out there, and here are my personal definitions of both loneliness and belonging :

Loneliness: *The feeling of loneliness is when you want to connect with someone, and there is no one to communicate with.*
Not belonging: *The sense of alienation and rejection that can happen when other people surround you.*

I believe that belonging counteracts loneliness, and in organizational terms, this means we can achieve our human potential to thrive in caring communities and beyond. When both requirements go unmet, these can trigger emotional and even physical harm and hurt.

Belonging goes beyond this, as it is about significant social relationships in general, rather than the need for attachment just with a primary caregiver.

Therefore, we are always looking to find and maintain the place where we belong. The effortlessness with which individuals become close to groups might show the deep force and power of this need. Interestingly, we are also deeply conditioned to provide a sense of belonging to others. The sense of belonging shapes the way our relationships function with others, groups, and even whole communities (Allen, Dr. Kelly-Ann).

Indeed, a sense of belonging is a state that manifests itself within a community while being measured on an individual basis. In a way, it can be described as the degree of identification and attachment the individual has to a reference group and its characteristics and values. The first place where we can develop this feeling is in our family, through a common name, rituals, traditions, and shared experiences.

How can we characterize this identification and attachment in the workplace? According to the participants in my research, it is when employees share the same values. When employees are happy to get up

---

[1] The need to connect: Acute social isolation causes neural craving responses similar to hunger L. Tomova, K. Wang, T. Thompson, G. Matthews, A. Takahashi, K. Tye, R. Saxedoi: https://doi.org/10.1101/2020.03.25.006643

in the morning to meet their colleagues and are motivated to face new challenges. In addition, it is when employees wear the organization brand like a badge of honor. Because when employees demonstrate a sense of pride in belonging to an organization, that is undoubtedly the feeling that we all want to have.

How Important Is Belonging?

Maslow's hierarchy of needs is the basis of the curriculum on motivation in most business schools. It is a remarkably robust theory, originally published in 1943, and proposes five human needs: physiological, safety, love and belonging, esteem, and self-actualization. These needs are represented in the form of a pyramid, with the more basic needs at the bottom.

Fundamental to understanding this theory is that the lower level needs should be adequately met before people can aspire to the higher needs. So, the *basic needs*—physiological needs such as food, water, warmth, and rest as well as safety, security, and health—are people's first concerns. Once it is no longer necessary to worry about meeting them, then people give more attention to what have been termed the *psychological needs*—love and belonging and esteem. Finally, people aspire to the *self-fulfillment needs*—self-actualization.

The model is not as simplistic or rigid as that. People are multi-motivated and Maslow himself later added cognitive, esthetic, and transcendence needs to his hierarchy (see Figure 2.1: Maslow's Hierarchy of Needs, p. 17).

The point of looking at it here, however, is to witness that the importance of *belonging* is a fundamental human need. It is also one of what Maslow called *deficiency needs*—people are motivated by this need when there is a deficit. This means that the need becomes stronger when people are denied it. Their attention is drawn to it, and their energies go into achieving it. This holds them back from achieving the higher-order needs—and particularly from self-actualization, where their energies would be given to becoming the best that they could be.

This is why this model is important for leaders to understand. When employees do not feel as if they are part of the organization, this becomes

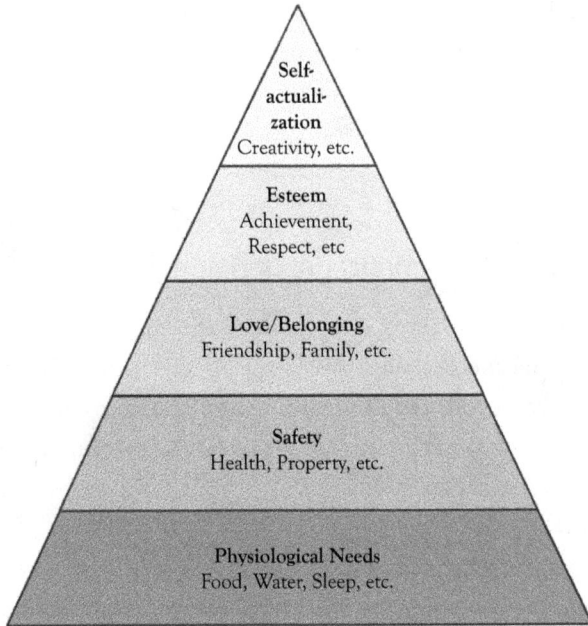

Figure 2.1 Maslow's hierarchy of needs

a driver for them to want it more. It becomes a distraction for them and literally holds them back from putting their energies into delivering the best work that they can.

In fact, the sense of nonbelonging is so real for many people that when I asked participants about their meaning of belonging, there was more of a description of what it felt like *not to belong*, as well as the impact that this has on their well-being.

In their 1995 paper, Baumeister and Leary[2] contended that we have underestimated the consequences of belonging. The need to belong appears to have multiple and substantial effects on both our emotional patterns and cognitive processes.

Neuroscientist Mathew Lieberman suggests that we never *turn off* our feelings about others and our relationships to them. Lieberman has shown that the default network for our brain when resting is identical to the neural, cognitive system that occurs when we participate in

---

[2] Baumeister, R.F., and Leary, M.R. 1995. *The Need to Belong: Desire for Interpersonal Attachments as a Fundamental Human Motivation*, p. 33.

group contact. This same default network has been measured in babies as young as two weeks, using functional magnetic resonance imaging. This provides evidence that we are indeed born to belong (Gao et al. 2009).

In the past years, there has been increased attention given to organizational belonging, focusing on teams and development of awareness, knowledge and skills about belonging.

Belonging and social disconnection often have a cultural, racial, or ethnicity base. Other bases may be age, gender, socioeconomic status, disability, sexual orientation, religion, and spirituality. Each grouping will have variances in facets of everyday life, family, and the role of individuals. Each of them can also act as a barrier to relationships, including relationships at work. This means that it is necessary to have some knowledge of other people's backgrounds for successful relationships to be established.

What Does This Mean for Organizations?

Well, if we are to learn from my research and other findings, it seems that freely discussing differences with others is a requirement for developing open and genuine relationships. Deliberate training about belonging, difference, and inclusion is necessary to achieve this.

This seems to be particularly important for white managers and employees. It has been shown that white people tend to regard themselves as *normal*, while others have a *race*. There is, therefore, a need for white managers and employees to have a stronger sense of self and a better understanding of past and present exploitations of other countries and races (Helms et al. 2009).

Deloitte's Global Human Capital Survey of business leaders found that the top two human capital trends are belonging and well-being, concepts that may speak to a greater sense of inclusion. Interestingly, 79 percent said belonging is important or very important for their company's success over the next 12 to 18 months, but only 13 percent said they are ready to address this trend.

At the same time, it is necessary to remember that people are not one-dimensional. While ethnicity, gender, and social class are identities that shape individual experiences, they are interconnected, and viewing them in isolation does not explain life's complexities. This means also that an individual belongs to more than one group—for example, his or her family, socio-professional group, sports group, and the company where he or she works.

Trust is at the base of much of this. We tend to place a higher initial trust with friends, family members, or people who share our way of thinking and behaving—we can perhaps term this affinity bias. The question is how to establish this trust within teams at work, because it is such a complex subject that touches people's very uniqueness.

We all need to make a measured effort to reserve that judgment and accept people if we want to build trust. To move forward, we may need to change many of our previous paradigms.

I believe people want to belong, be needed, and feel valued, and our longing to assimilate may force us to conceal who we indeed are. But, when we are respected and included *because of* or *regardless of* what makes us different, we feel both safety and belonging.

A recent study by My Kinda Future[3] found that, for U.K. office workers, salary remained the number one workplace perk. However, cultural attributes—feeling valued and getting on with colleagues—were significantly more important to them than the other traditional monetary incentives that employers so often invest in. These included perks such as subsidized gyms, office parties, and health insurance. Again, the EY Belonging Barometer of 2018, which surveyed American workers, found that employees across all generations said *checking in* with employees, that is, asking how they are, finding out how they are doing on a personal level, did more to make them feel that they belonged than the traditional actions of feedback on performance, public recognition, being invited to out-of-office events, being asked to join meetings with senior leaders, or being included on e-mails with senior leaders.

Belonging is vital for our emotional and physical health and plays a big part in the way we reason and cooperate with the world. The way we engage with others is fundamental to our civilization.

---

[3] Creating Belonging in a Digital Age: https://mykindafuture.com/2020/03/30/creating-belonging-in-a-digital-age/

> **Reflective Exercise**
>
> How do you signal the importance of belonging?
>
> - *Notice it:* Observe the belonging signals you send out.
> - *Ask yourself honestly:* How frequently do I notice all team members, personally and professionally?
> - *Name it:* Label how to signal the belonging cues you could be sending each other. Ask: Do I regularly create an accessible and inclusive environment where all people belong?
> - *Nail it:* Practice sending those gestures daily. Ask: Do I build people up, lift them, and allow them to belong truly?

Findings and Quotes From My Research

How Participants Defined Belonging

The overall finding from my research was that participants defined belonging in terms of social relationships based on inclusion, acceptance, and recognition.

For the participants, the sense of belonging accords with the human need to make connections with other people. This connection is possible when they share the same interests, goals, values, language, beliefs, hopes, concerns, and/or traditions. When *strong* social relationships are established, this craving for belonging can be satisfied.

The sense of belonging, thus, implies personal identification with the group. It is through belonging to a group that people define their identity.

> *[Belonging] implies personal identification with the group, the adoption of its values, norms and habits, and the feeling of solidarity with those who also belong to it. A sense of belonging [is] an interactive process by which individuals are interrelated and define themselves with each other according to fields of interest and affinity.*
> —Psychotherapist, Medical Centre

Inclusion within a group allows its members to feel affection and support. Participants used words like love and esteem to describe the feeling that being in a group generates.

Belonging to a group or community allows us to obtain affection and love. The group also allows us to express ourselves, to have a place and a role, to listen, to be supported. It allows us to structure our identity and to affirm our own existence.
                    —Professor of Leadership, Executive Education

A sense of belonging mitigates against loneliness. This is related to the need to have support from other members of the group in times of difficulty.

When you're having a tough day or struggling with something, imagine a friend or family member coming to you and asking how you are. That's belonging.
                    —Legal Director, Multinational

[Belonging] means that you can count on their help in case you need it.
                    —Neuroscientist

Participants also referred to a feeling of *security* that is generated by the acceptance received from group members. Being heard and respected means that they are accepted and can be *free* to be as they are. Recognizing differences within the group and welcoming them is part of this process. People do not want to be rejected.

[Belonging] is feeling you can be yourself, and you are loved, welcomed.
                    —Personal Stylist, Fashion and Beauty Industry

Belonging means that I feel safe, loved and desired for just being who I am. I don't have to change anything about myself, don't have to conform to what others want me to be, I can just be free to live the way God has made me to be.
                    —Business Unit Head, Energy

Having stable social relationships and being part of a group where they feel loved, safe and accepted, generates happiness and better health. This acts as a source of resilience, solidarity and loyalty. Thus, group members become a resource in times of stress.

A sense of belonging to a greater community improves your motivation, health, and happiness. When you see your connection to others, you know that all people struggle and have difficult times. You are not alone. There is comfort in that knowledge.

—HR VP, Airline Industry

There are multiple groups in which a sense of belonging can be developed; participants mention family, school, the circle of friends, workplace, church, and real or virtual communities, including on social media.

There are some special connotations associated with a sense of belonging in the workplace. When the participants referred to the sense of belonging in an organization, some highlighted that a friendly relationship with their co-workers is a more significant motivator than working conditions, money, and work itself.

Management, working conditions, environment, remuneration, organization; none of them really give employees satisfaction like the statement, 'I have a good friend at work' gives satisfaction.

—Audit Partner, Law Sector

There is an affective component to the sense of belonging in an organization. Having had social relationships at work, or not having friends, becomes a source of unhappiness and hurts both mental and physical health.

Not having good relations with colleagues decreases an employee's sense of happiness, and it can spoil everything.

—Project Manager, Real Estate

Sharing personal experiences at work helps build empathy between individuals. Some participants described the satisfaction they felt when co-workers were interested in knowing about the well-being of their families. Some also noted how friendly relationships in the workplace were beneficial to their personal lives.

Sometimes professional recognition helps to overcome difficult moments in private life

—Head of Legal, Perfume Industry

Good relationships in the workplace also motivate and create a sense of security. When individuals feel that they will have support from their co-workers, it encourages them to speak up and share their ideas.

Participants indicated that a vital element for individuals to feel included and accepted in the workplace is recognition associated with the role they have in the organization.

> *What makes me feel like I'm part of the team is when I'm doing a treatment on a patient and the next day the colleagues tell me that my protocol worked well, healing or whatever; I'm satisfied. It's the fact that my work is valued, the recognition I get. That increases my sense of belonging.*
>
> —University Philosophy Professor, Education

CHAPTER 3

Inclusion and Exclusion

There are biases conscious and unconscious that have to be rooted out.
——Barack Obama

Inclusion is a state of being valued, respected, and supported. It is about focusing on the needs of every individual and ensuring the right conditions are in place for each person to achieve his or her full potential. Inclusion should be reflected in an organization's culture and in the practices and relationships that are in place to support a diverse workforce.

A study reported in "Does Rejection Hurt? An fMRI Study of Social Exclusion" (Eisenberger, NI 2003) describes revolutionary research in social neuroscience that exposes that our need to bond with other people is even more crucial than our need for food or shelter. Furthermore, the social pain and pleasure we experience have the same underlying neural processes as physical pain and pleasure.

What is it that gets in the way of bonding with others and being included into social or work groups? Some of the key factors seem to be bias, stereotyping, and lack of self-awareness.

Perhaps, most important is to recognize that much of the basis for stereotypes, prejudices, and final exclusion of others has to do with ego:

The ego needs to feel superior; it needs to be right and will look for evidence to support its assumptions. A genuine relationship is one that is not dominated by the ego, and the truth needs no defense.

—Eckart Tolle

Unconscious Bias

Bias is defined as an inclination either toward or against an idea, person, or group, very often in a way that is seen to be unfair. While we can accept that as a theory, it is surprising how many of us deny having any biases of our own.

The expert on biases is Daniel Kahneman[1], a psychologist who has also been awarded a Nobel Prize in economics. He has shown that we are permanently subject to what is called cognitive bias, that is, errors of reasoning. These errors constantly interfere with our logic as we try to make sense of the world around us or make important decisions.

Biases are useful to us when we need to make quick decisions—they are often what we might term *rules of thumb* to simplify information processing and help us know what we should remember. The truth is that there really is too much information in the world, and we have to filter some of it out. Our brains try to pick out the bits that are likely to be useful—but this means that important information can also be filtered out. We also tend to notice things that are related to other things that have already been loaded into our memories. Or we notice things that are unusual or surprising. And, we are drawn to information that confirms our own existing beliefs. You will probably have heard about *confirmation bias* or *congruence bias*.

The problem is that most of these biases are unconscious—we have no idea we have them. So, we think we are making logical, objective judgments and decisions, but we may be tripped up by biases that will lead to bad decisions. For example, there is an *influence and persuasion bias*—well-spoken ideas are disproportionately valued, while less strongly presented ideas are undervalued. There is also *hierarchy bias*, where we confuse position with expertise. And, what about *attachment bias*, where we place a high value on our own ideas? And, *uncertainty aversion*, where we tend to respond negatively to uncertainty, triggering avoidance and fear behaviors. *Self-service bias* is about blaming external forces when something goes wrong and giving yourself credit when good things happen. And, unfortunately, we have the *Dunning–Kruger effect*, where you think that you are smarter and more capable than you actually are, and you cannot recognize your own incompetence.

---

[1] Thinking Fast and Slow Daniel Kahneman Project Implicit was founded in 1998 by three scientists—Tony Greenwald (University of Washington), Mahzarin Banaji (Harvard University), and Brian Nosek (University of Virginia).

There are several hundred identified biases. Some of the preceding examples may help to explain how powerful they are, and you may start to imagine the impact they may have.

A form of bias is the tendency of human beings to place individuals into social categories. These groupings are based on visual cues such as gender, cultural background, age, height, or body size. We additionally catalog people around their social context, professional roles, religious distinctiveness, or political affiliation.

Princeton psychologist Alexander Todorov notes how little information we need to make up our minds. He and his team presented a photo of someone to a group for 100 milliseconds, 500 milliseconds, then up to a full second. They then asked people to make various judgments. What they found is that you do not need more than a 200-millisecond exposure to a facial image to make a judgment; 200 milliseconds are a single-glance impression. The issue with first impressions shaping so much of our lives is that we do not see them as a problem, says Professor Todorov. "People know there are lots of biases based on sexual orientation, based on race and other factors, once you're aware of these, you can create a policy that prevents discrimination. If you think first impressions are just fine and accurate, we have a problem. They go unacknowledged, 'underneath the table.'"

Irrespective of difference, we all have central human needs and emotions. In life and work, it is vital and valuable to acknowledge these differences. How we have the conversation about the difference may be uncomfortable, and I have seen in my work with inclusion and belonging, it always creates deeper authentic relationships.

> Blind spots and biases impact our awareness of ourselves.
> Anytime a trait is hard for us to see, hear, accept. It's a blind spot.

Implicit Bias Tests

One effective way to explore our bias is that Mahzarin R. Banaji developed the Implicit Bias Tests (IAT). Banaji is a professor of psychology at Harvard University and coauthor of *Blindspot*, along with Anthony Greenwald and Brian Nosek. These tests were created to help people recognize unconscious bias, and now they are being used by companies to help employees understand that hidden biases are real. The battery of tests can be taken in approximately 10 minutes and can be modified to assess unconscious bias in different categories, for example, whether white test-takers are likelier to associate *good* words with white faces more quickly than with black faces. (They are, and black test-takers show the reverse results.)

Project Implicit is a nonprofit organization and international collaboration between researchers who are interested in implicit social cognition—thoughts and feelings outside of conscious awareness and control. The goal of the organization is to educate the public about hidden biases and to provide a *virtual laboratory* for collecting data on the Internet.

The IAT measures the strength of associations between concepts (e.g., black people, gay people) and evaluations (e.g., good, bad) or stereotypes (e.g., athletic, clumsy). The main idea is that making a response is easier when closely related items share the same response key. It is not meant to embarrass people; instead, it asks what steps we could take to improve the situation. One thing for sure is that these types of experiences act as collective filters when we make assessments and judgments of people around us. Besides this, research tells us that human beings have a natural tendency to place individuals into social classifications, and these groupings are often based on visual cues such as gender, cultural background, age, height, and body size.

We catalog people based on their social context, professional roles, race, gender, religious distinctiveness, and political affiliation. Bias is the preferences we make that are formed in childhood, through our education, are often a mishmash of all our experiences that come together to form our predispositions and preferences.

Racism comes in many forms; sometimes, it is blatant and associated with extreme violence, as we have all witnessed. However, in the workplace, it is more obscure and insidious.

Take It at Face Value

In *Face Value: The Irresistible Influence of First Impressions*, Alexander Todorov begins with this story about how faces might even influence the outcome of elections.

Alexander Todorov is one of the world's leading researchers on how we are influenced by each other's faces. When people do not believe that they have a scrap of preference, uprooting the bias becomes very difficult to tackle. We do, we all do, and we are all too quick to categorize people instead of identifying what skills people bring to the table. Unconscious bias is deeply rooted and often surfaces when we are multitasking or when we are stressed, as research[2] shows. It comes up in tense situations when we do not have time to think, and we try to make snap decisions. It is part of our evolutionary fight-or-flight response. It is automatic. We all have stereotypes that we are not aware of. Becoming aware of unconscious bias and then ignoring how it shows up in our daily life is a disastrous practice. The challenge is to be realistic and not to pretend to eliminate biases, but to try to interrupt them so that we can behave in ways that are aligned with our values.

Working against the odds is hard enough, so lifting each other is the only way we are going to advance. When someone has your back, believes in you, and provides a safe place for you to thrive, who knows what you can do? We must not separate but celebrate each other. Be the ally and call it out.

Silence gives consent to bad behavior, and we are all accountable and responsible.

Project Implicit[3] is a nonprofit organization and international collaboration between researchers who are interested in implicit social cognition—thoughts and feelings outside of conscious awareness and control. The goal of the organization is to educate the public about hidden biases and to provide a *virtual laboratory* for collecting data on the Internet.

Todorov's work illustrates how quickly we make impressions, and how these judgments can generate in- and out-group behavior and eventually lead to a lack of belonging. These first impressions may not be precise, but

---

[2] Office of Diversity and Outreach University of San Francisco, DiversityOutreach@ucsf.edu.

[3] Xu, X, X. Zuo, X. Wang, and S. Han. July 1, 2009. "Do you Feel My Pain? Racial Group Membership Modulates Empathic Neural Responses." *Journal of Neuroscience* 29, no. 26. pp. 8525–8529.

they can be ongoing and uncomfortably demonstrate the mistakes in and fundamental injustice of many of our decisions.

However, these biased categorizations are generally unintended. The unconscious people preferences we have are formed in childhood were played out in education and are a melting pot of all our experiences. So, for example, if we keep seeing males in positions of authority or power, something gets triggered in the unconscious brain, and this becomes our expectation, unless we start seeing females in positions of authority or power. I came from a background where, in my childhood home, men's voices were more significant than women's, and somehow this stayed with me unconsciously until it showed up in my IAT results.

If for all your life you have been exposed, consciously and unconsciously, to the message that white skin is beautiful you will automatically make this association, and it will impact your decision making and your choices. It is only when you become aware that you can slow the process down.

A powerful example of unconscious bias in action was highlighted by Jane Lazarre in her book *Beyond the Whiteness of Whiteness: Memoir of a White Mother of Black Sons*. She gives a very personal account of racial disparity in the medical treatment of her son. Indeed, an increasing body of research suggests that doctors' unconscious behavior plays a role in practice and care. Numerous findings show that African American patients are often prescribed less pain medication than white patients with the same complaints. Black patients with chest pain are referred for advanced cardiac care less often than white patients with identical symptoms.

This type of behavior becomes difficult to deal with when people do not believe that they have these preferences and think that they are somehow immune to bias. The truth is that we all have them, and we are all quick to sort and categorize people and make judgments without first identifying what skills people bring to the table. If we can become aware of our biases, we will be better able to decide whether we believe they are accurate or not and whether we should hold onto them or dismiss them.

What is important here is that belonging and bias are opposing forces. Our unconscious biases impact our behaviors and decisions. They are not merely involuntary individual preferences that are formed by socialization and personal experiences.

Having worked all around the world does not come without its challenges, and even though I believe I am open-minded, I am human, and I have had to examine my own unconscious biases and dig deeper into how they were affecting my behavior. When I facilitate, I focus on different forms of unconscious bias that can prevent us from cultivating an inclusive and innovative workplace. The goal is to help us all recognize our biases so that we can limit the adverse effects in the workplace.

Prejudice and Stereotyping

Closely associated with biases are stereotypes and prejudices. And they are powerful tools for exclusion and *us/them* thinking.

Stereotyping

Stereotyping is the tendency to look at people not as individuals but as part of groups. This is part of the social categorization discussed earlier. Certain characteristics of these groups are exaggerated, and judgments are made based on these characteristics. The result is generally a blurred judgment as differences and information are excluded and individual verification is not done. Stereotyping does not have to be negative, but there is a tendency for favorable tendencies to be either omitted or not stressed. Examples of positive stereotypes might include notions like overweight people are *jolly*, women are warm and communal, African Americans are athletic, Asians have better math ability.

However, there are also negative stereotypes, and often even the positive stereotypes have a negative association. So, women may be warm, but they are also weak. Asians can do math but are cold. African Americans are athletic but unintelligent.

Obviously, all of these stereotypes are "in the eye of the beholder", so to speak. People tend to see themselves in a certain way, and others as different. However, stereotypes are often generally known by members of groups and may influence the way they think about themselves too.

Prejudice

Prejudice is generally a negative attitude toward members of some group, based only on their membership of that group. The group as a whole is seen as inferior, and derogatory stereotypes are developed. People are pre-judged, and any inconsistent information is screened out. Membership of our own social groups helps form our identity, and prejudice is common against members of an unfamiliar cultural group.

The way that we see the world creates our perspective on a situation. In a paper called *Do You Feel My Pain?* Xiaojing Xu et al[4] showed that empathy by racial group association plays a pivotal role in shaping social behaviors. For example, they found that people's unconscious responses to simple emotions in others varied according to whether the others were of the same race or not. Hence, the Chinese reacted more to photos of Chinese injury and whites to white injury.

I have observed in many facilitation sessions that talking about par-ticular stereotypes or prejudices leads to disconnection. Debating *uncon-scious bias* is a better way of connecting people.

Self-Awareness Is a Superpower

Self-awareness is the foundation of personal growth and success. Daniel Goleman calls it the *keystone* of emotional intelligence; indeed, build-ing self-awareness is a life-long effort. Interestingly, when I talk about self-awareness in my work with clients, I see eyes roll, and I have to remind the cynics that self-awareness is a *soft skill* that translates into hard results in organizations. Daniel Goleman reminds us that "self-awareness isn't just navel-gazing. It's the presence of mind to be flexible in how you respond. Besides, it allows you to be centered and know what your body is telling you." Self-awareness is the means or the ability to monitor our inner world—our thoughts and feelings.

Google has built a whole learning movement called *Search inside Your-self*[5] using the tools of neuroscience, mindfulness, and emotional intel-ligence. SIYL provides evidence-based practices for leaders to grow, to

[4] Xu, X., X. Zuo, X. Wang, and S. Han. July 1, 2009. "Do you Feel My Pain? Racial Group Membership Modulates Empathic Neural Responses." *Journal of Neuroscience* 29, no. 26. pp. 8525–8529.

[5] Search Inside Yourself - Leadership Institute, www.siyli.org/siy, developed at Google, based on neuroscience.

become more self-aware, and to become better leaders. Self-awareness is central because when we have a greater understanding of ourselves and consequently can experience ourselves as separate individuals, this enables us to build on our areas of strength as well as to detect areas where we would like to make developments.

Self-awareness is especially important for those managing diverse teams. Understanding the different expectations and behavioral customs that others may have compared to your own is a big step toward establishing trust and proactively building relationships.

Equally helpful is curiosity and genuine interest in other people and what makes them different. When successful teams leverage difference, this is energizing for team members rather than exhausting. However, we cannot be complacent and research[6] shows that diverse teams when managed correctly are successful. And, as for anything in life, we all have to nurture and maintain appropriate conscious behavior. We need to be honest with ourselves and each other about the reality of our biases and beliefs and how they impact our behavior, our relationships, and our lives. When we find ourselves blaming the other person, we need to look inward to try to identify the unconscious bias that may be driving us.

I feel so very privileged to have had an opportunity in my lifetime to talk about what diversity means, what it looks like, what it feels like, and how we can help each other in going forward just by being more aware of our behavior, our actions, and our stereotypes. Indeed, stereotypes are often automatic and unconscious. At work, stereotypes can influence decisions we make about other people, preventing their ability to contribute to their jobs entirely. I know that to be true from my own professional experience and as a leadership coach.

The feeling of belonging is one of the elements of identity and the sense of self. Indeed, according to sociologist Guy Rocher, "Belonging to a community means sharing with other members enough ideas or common traits to recognize oneself in the 'we'" (Rocher 1968).

The sense of belonging is never in isolation. To be able to share ideas with other members, the individual must first be accepted and recognized

---

[6] *Why Diverse Teams Are Smarter* by David Rock and Heidi Grant November 04, 2016.

by them. And, according to JC Turner, "...membership in a particular group is related to a positive evaluation of its attributes in comparison with other groups."

Granted, there are also moments in life where we take a step back from some of the groups to which we belong. This has happened in my life when belonging to a specific group began to feel less comfortable. I firstly started to question the meaning of the group, then I started to criticize it, and then finally, sometimes I wanted to leave it.

The desire to join a new group leads people to the idea that something will have to be changed in the way they are, act, and perhaps think. To improve groups and to facilitate integration into the new one, the individual takes the risk of no longer conforming with the group to which they currently belong.

However, as Aebischer and Oberlé (1998) point out, "Reference groups provide us with benchmarks for comparison that allow us to evaluate ourselves; they offer us norms and models that influence our attitudes and opinions... Sometimes, however, comparison with groups other than those to which we belong leads to the opposite result: it confirms that this or that group to which we belong is indeed a group we care about, that is important to us, to which we want to continue to refer."

Belonging is the desire for close relationships, for feeling part of a group, being free to express troubles because that group accepts you. People have a compelling need to belong and be included, and the pain of being excluded is something we can all connect with, wherever we are from and whatever we do.

Reflective Exercise

Think back to a time when you did not feel included. Was it at school, college, in a sports team, a party?

1. Briefly describe this event. How did it make you feel?
2. Think back to a time and identify a moment when you did something to fit in with a group.
   a. What did you do to belong?
   b. When can it be useful to accommodate to belong to a group?
   c. When can conformity be harmful?

Findings and Quotes From My Research

Challenges for Organizations

There are a number of challenges that leaders and organizations will face in trying to establish an environment of inclusion and belonging. These include the pressure to accommodate a diverse workforce, generational differences, managing remote work, and the need to have a management style that considers the emotions of individuals.

Appreciating Diversity

Participants believed that drawing on a diversity of backgrounds, experiences, skills, cultures, nationalities, and gender created opportunities, new ideas, and better results. However, maintaining a diverse environment is also a challenge.

Organizations are expected to guarantee equal opportunities, combat biases, promote tolerance and acceptance, strengthen ties, create a collective identity around the same purpose, and create an environment where each individual, regardless of origins or beliefs, feels included and part of the group. Diversity must be valued individually, and this is not an easy task.

Participants agreed that diverse groups can be more intelligent, creative, and useful. They are a source of enrichment. Diversity creates opportunities for innovation and growth; it is essential for organizations, so it is vital to develop an inclusive culture, where individuals feel motivated to give their best.

Participants suggested that it takes more than just recognizing differences to create an environment where individuals feel free and comfortable to be themselves, where they can feel authentic, recognized, and respected for who they are, with their strengths and weaknesses. It is about appreciating these differences.

> *Organizations still need to capitalize on a greater diverse workforce and create the right environment where differences become an asset that leads to creativity, idea generation and, ultimately, innovation.*
> —President, Hospitality Industry

Language and nationality created barriers and led to the lack of sense of belonging experienced by some participants.

> *I find it difficult as a non-native speaker to be heard in office interactions. I often refrain from contributing because I feel I do not speak as 'powerfully' as my native counterparts and don't belong to their club.*
> —Company Owner, Real Estate

> *I was a Managing Director of the Indian subsidiary of a multinational engineering company; I managed a team of close to 100 people. I have observed a great tendency in people to believe the people of certain nationalities more. For example, a person from the European management will listen and believe a junior, inexperienced European person much more than an experienced or senior local person from the subsidiary office. This made me feel that I did not belong and was not included.*
> —Deputy Head, Primary Education

Several participants highlighted that gender diversity represents a unique advantage for organizations. Women create opportunities to learn, are a source of creativity and innovation, and can create a healthy environment for all. However, there is a challenge for many organizations to improve on the low representation of women in leadership positions.

One of the participants spoke about her experience as a mother and leader and highlights a particular challenge for women in organizations:

> *I had to figure out how to balance my role as a leader with my mom status, including how to find time for all the things that come after giving birth. Hint: several of them were too uncomfortable to talk about at the office! Like racing home if my baby got sick. Or leaving a little early to take him to the doctor.*
> —Project Manager, Construction Industry

In those organizations where inclusion and respect for diversity are promoted, policies to combat discrimination have been their main tool. However, one participant pointed out that research suggests that anti-bias programs rarely work. Rather, it is the role of the leader to make all voices heard.

Globalization provides enormous opportunities for corporations, but on an individual level, there are challenges. Technical competencies in one area are no longer enough to succeed in a global environment. Being aware and acknowledging how others function in another culture are paramount for building trust and respect.

—Diversity and Inclusion Officer, Tech Industry

Rather than relying on the policies and anti-bias programs, organizations should focus on creating a collective identity that gives individuals something to have in common, despite a diversity of ideas, culture, and beliefs.

Every company is made up of social groups and individuals belonging to one or more nationalities, regions and professional cultures. To ensure coherence, the company must create a collective identity, which will become the common point of all its members.

—CEO, Communications Industry

Accommodating Generations Y–Z

The new generations of workers also bring new challenges for organizations. For Generation Y (millennials, born between 1981 and 1996) and Generation Z (born between 1997 and 2015), the meaning of work and happiness within the organization is very important.

The company must be able to welcome the famous Y-Z generations whose happiness at work is an important criterion in their job search.

—Director of Operations, Telecoms

[We] are participating in a re-founding of the world of work based on agility and mobility - changes of trajectory, retraining, teleworking, freelance jobs, etc. Because when we are in search of meaning, we move, explore, evolve, deconstruct, and rebuild.

—Monk, Self-Development Industry

Some estimate that the youngest workers last on average 12 to 18 months in a company. If organizations want to attract and, above all, retain these talents, it is vital that they develop trust-based management and foster a sense of belonging. A participant points out that it is not about a communication strategy or monetary incentives, but rather about creating inclusive environments that welcome these new generations. It is about building loyalty to retain them in the organization.

> *Belonging, fitting in, (whatever you want to call it), in organizations is necessary for the millennial generation. They need to create impact quickly, and they need feedback to know what they do matters. Today's young people stay in a company for an average of twelve to eighteen months, creating some instability in organizations. As a result, to give this generation the desire to stay, organizations will have to be agile, adapt, transform. One of the adjustments is to create a genuine sense of belonging. This shift is hard to implement and so overdue.*
>
> —Global Diversity Officer, Consulting

Belonging and Disagreement

Part of the diversity to be encouraged in groups is cognitive diversity—different ways of thinking, different approaches to problems, different opinions, different thinking styles and levels.

One of the results of this type of diversity, however, is disagreement. Differences between individuals should be valued and, in the event of a conflict, respect and dignity are called for. Criticism must be seen as constructive, there to help solve a problem.

This is only possible in teams where members trust, support, and respect each other. They have confidence in each other's ability to do their work to the best of their ability. This allows for open conversations when there is disagreement. What we do not want in teams is the feeling that differences become conflicts, and that some people abuse the power that they have, as expressed by a participant in my research:

> *I feel powerlessness. Any confrontations with my boss left me always being on the losing side.*
>
> —VP Pharma

CHAPTER 4

Relationships

It's always about people.... always
—David O Russell, Film Director.

The first group to which the individual belongs is the family. Later, there is a progression from a relationship of attachment within the family to developing a network of friendships through belonging to other groups. When our social needs are met, we feel accepted, loved, appreciated and, conversely, not alone or rejected. These are attitudes or even actions that can be undertaken either by the person wanting to join and be accepted by a group and also by people who are trying to make it easier for others to be included and accepted.

We are social beings and being part of groups is part of being social. This may sound obvious, but there is more to this statement than meets the eye. There is an immeasurable amount written about relationships. I want to concentrate here on the pieces that I think are helpful in building relationships and where the goal is belonging.

Being Social Is for Survival

According to Dr. Martin Juneau[1], a cardiologist at the Montreal Heart Institute, social isolation increases the risk of dying prematurely, just as obesity, sedentary lifestyle, or smoking increases the risk of death. Conversely, a quality social network would make it easier to cope with the

---

[1] Dr Martin Juneau Social isolation: An important risk factor for premature death Social determinants of mental health. 1. Mental Health. 2. Socioeconomic Factors. 3. Mental Disorders—prevention and control. I. World Health Organization. ISBN 978 92 4 150680 9 (NLM classification: WM 101), World Health Organization, 2014.

stress caused by life's trials and tribulations, thereby reducing the risk factors for mental and physical health.

In his book, *Tribe: On Homecoming and Belonging*, Sebastian Junger explains what tribal societies teach us about belonging. Junger advocates that belonging is valuable because we are primates, and all primate species are social. He contends that we are social for an excellent reason because we are vulnerable, and we require the security of the group to mature to adulthood. Protection is more manageable in groups, as solitary primates, including humans, cannot survive in the wild.

> *We do need each other. We believe of ourselves as an extremely superior species, but we hold psychological necessities, emotional needs, that are only served by a group. And so, we search for belonging because we're wired for it, because it's an adaptation that leads to survival—Sebastian Junger.*

According to Junger, the three things that human beings need to be content are "to feel competent at what they do, to feel authentic in their lives and to feel connected to others."

This is true of organizations too. If we do not have it, things start to go awry. Research shows that in modern society, when we begin to lose that sense of belonging, suicide rates rise, depression rates increase, and mental illness cases go up[2]. So, there is an explicit humanistic cost, the cost of not belonging, in a prosperous present-day organization.

Organizations are like families, symbiotic with all the small parts. There are separate entities inside a family or in organization, and any modification, big, small, good, bad, in one part directly influences the entire system. And, we need to be mindful of the interactions.

The Strength of Weak Relationships

What may be quite surprising is that our social needs and our need for connection and belonging are not dependent only on strong or close relationships.

---

[2] Social Interactions and Well-Being: The Surprising Power of Weak Ties Gillian M. Sandstrom, Elizabeth W. Dunn, First Published April 25, 2014.

Psychologist Elizabeth Dunn and her collaborator Gillian M. Sand-strom[3] examined whether short conversations with strangers could lift moods. They requested participants to enter a bustling coffee shop and buy a drink. Half of the participants would get in and get out of the coffee shop, and the other half would strike up a dialogue with the cashier. They discovered that people who turned this economic transaction into a quick social interaction left the shop in a better mood and felt a greater sense of belonging in their community.

That episode inspired Sandstrom to investigate the extent to which people derive happiness from weak-tie relationships. She asked a group of respondents to keep a record of all their social interactions over several days.

Sandstorm found that participants with more extensive networks of weak ties tended to be happier overall, and on days when participants had a more significant number of casual interactions with weak links, they experienced more happiness and a greater sense of belonging.

What Sandstorm's research demonstrates is that while close links are important, making networks of casual connections can increase happiness and a sense of belonging.

This finding is similar to that of Mark Granovetter[4], a sociology professor at Stanford University, in his 1973 paper titled *The Strength of Weak Ties*. He contended that working societies are underpinned not only by *strong ties* (close relationships) but also by *weak ties* (casual acquaintances). Where strong ties favor dense, overlapping networks, weak links connect us to a more extensive and more diverse group of people. What Granovetter showed is that quantity matters, too.

Granovetter examined 282 Boston-based workers and observed that most of them got their jobs through someone they knew. However, only a minority got the job through a close friend, while 84 percent got their job through a weak-tie relationship—casual contacts whom they saw only occasionally. Granovetter concluded from his research that the more of

[3] "The Strength of Weak Ties: A Network Theory Revisited Granovetter." *Sociological Theory* 1, pp. 201–233, WILEY AND SONS.
[4] (Organizational Behavior, June 2003) Thesis Title: To Speak or Not to Speak: The Multi-Level Leadership Influences on Voice and Silence in Organizations.

these acquaintances we have, the better. His work showed that we also get much of our new information from weak links. That provides stimulation but also, in a time of uncertainty, guidance on how to behave. From a systemic view, this means that establishing bonds with others, however weak, is essential for the whole organization.

Increased Sense of Meaning

In a 2016 study, which included respondents from Italy and Scotland[5], psychologists showed that, regardless of nationality or age, people who were members of groups such as sports teams or church communities enjoyed an increased sense of meaning and security. And, the more groups of which they were members, the better.

The conclusions imply that thinking more about one's group life could have meaningful gains for one's overall sense of happiness. While this conclusion might appear rather instinctive, it touches something that is deep within all of us: to be our best selves, we need the help of others.

Group Dynamics

Wilfred Bion, a psychoanalyst working with troops during the Second World War, was one of the founders of group dynamics. He made some interesting observations, most importantly that the group took on its own dynamic, separate from the individuals who were its members. There were also basic assumptions that underpinned some of these groups that led to them functioning poorly and distracting them from their original purpose. He called these assumptions *dependency*, *fight-flight*, and *pairing*.

Understanding these assumptions—that group members are generally unaware of—may help to explain what is happening in some groups and why they are basically dysfunctional.

Dependency: In groups where dependency is the underlying assumption, we tend to find feelings of helplessness, inadequacy, neediness, and fear. Members are always looking for a leader who will somehow protect them, guide them, and *save* them from their own anxieties. Individuals

---

[5] BBC work life why your 'weak-tie' friendships may mean more than you think.

tend to suspend critical judgment on issues, and there is generally a lack of individual initiative.

Fight-flight: These groups are involved in avoidance and attack—with other groups and even internally. There is a tendency to us/them thinking and taking sides. For those who experience the fight reaction, there are feelings of aggression, jealousy, competition, and rivalry. The flight group shows avoidance, absenteeism, giving up. These groups often are distracted from whatever brought them together originally into fighting lost causes.

Pairing: Some groups decide that the best way to solve problems is through smaller groups of two. A typical comment will be, "Just leave it to the two of us." Unfortunately, this generally leads to splitting of the group and increased inter- and intra-group conflict. This approach is often tried in work teams.

It is important also to understand Bion's definition of a *work group culture*. This is where the structures and behaviors of the group support and facilitate the attainment of group goals and also satisfy the needs of individual members. When a group is operating in this mode, concentrating on tasks and objectives, the communication within the group is likely to be open and honest, guided by rational thought. It is when something goes wrong and people start to experience fear or anxiety, that the group then *regresses* into its assumptive culture—one of the three described earlier.

If you are a people manager or leader in an organization, it is very likely that you have, at some stage, been at a loss to understand what is going on in some of your teams. Sometimes, a theoretical model, such as Bion's, can be very useful for helping you to recognize the symptoms of dysfunction.

Equally, as an individual, with a great longing for belonging, it is sometimes a good idea to step back from the group you are so wanting to be part of, to decide whether or not membership would really benefit you. When a group is not functioning well, it may be necessary to remove yourself from it.

A further word of caution may be necessary. While belonging is a fundamental need, we aspire to belong ourselves, and we are encouraged to help others to belong, there is a danger that belonging can actually cause separation.

Sometimes, we derive such a sense of purpose from belonging to a particular group that we separate from those who are not part of it. This might be quite subtle, when people speak differently, have different educational backgrounds or have different beliefs, and we might dismiss or ignore them because they do not belong where we belong.

We might choose to be separated from certain groups, but we may also be cutting ourselves off from potential benefits, learning, and support. It is useful to be watchful about whether our need to belong to a particular group translates into a refusal to accept someone with whom we align elsewhere.

Reflective Exercise

According to Cornell Professor James Detert[6], getting employees to speak freely can be especially difficult, largely due to workplace norms, along with their fear of losing out on bonuses, promotions, and even their jobs for speaking up.

Here is an is exercise that may serve as a starting point to identifying how open the conversations are in your team and how well you are using them to encourage belonging and to deal with disagreements.

Start by asking and answering these questions, this could be an individual exercise or a team exercise.

1. Is it risky to disagree with others or give candid feedback to your peers?
2. When you make a mistake, can you talk about it openly?
3. Are you risking belonging to the group if you speak your mind?
4. Is there blaming and shaming going on?
5. Is your team a hostage to harmony?

Whichever techniques you may choose to adopt, empathy is the ability to recognize, understand, and share the feelings of another person. You put yourself in someone else's shoes and see the situation or world through the eyes of that person.

---

[6] Can Your Employees Really Speak Freely?
Despite their best intentions, managers tend to shut people down. by James R. Detert and Ethan Burris HBR From the Magazine (January–February 2016).

Findings and Quotes From My Research

Social Relationships Belonging, Acceptance, and Recognition

For the participants, the sense of belonging accords with the human need to make connections with other people. This connection is possible when they share the same interests, goals, values, language, beliefs, hopes, concerns, or traditions. When *strong* social relationships are established, this craving for belonging can be satisfied.

> *None of us can belong to all the groups we'd like to, but it is essential that we feel we belong somewhere and have some connections.*
> —VP Oncology, Pharma

The sense of belonging thus implies personal identification with the group. It is through belonging to a group that people define their identity.

> *[Belonging] implies personal identification with the group, the adoption of its values, norms and habits, and the feeling of solidarity with those who also belong to it. A sense of belonging [is] an interactive process by which individuals are interrelated and define themselves with each other according to fields of interest and affinity.*
> Psychotherapist, Medical Centre

Inclusion within a group allows its members to feel affection and support. Participants used words like love and esteem to describe the feeling that being in a group generates.

> *To me, belonging means that I feel safe, loved. I want my children to have that sense of belonging. I want them always to feel like they are loved, appreciated and safe.*
> —Director Business Unit, Energy Industry

> *Belonging to a group or community allows us to obtain affection and love. The group also allows us to express ourselves, to have a place and a role, to listen, to be supported. It allows us to structure our identity and to affirm our own existence.*
> —Professor of Leadership, Executive Education

A sense of belonging mitigates against loneliness. This is related to the need to have support from other members of the group in times of difficulty.

> *When you're having a tough day or struggling with something, imagine a friend or family member coming to you and asking how you are. That's belonging.*
>
> —Legal Director, Multinational

> *[Belonging] means that you can count on their help in case you need it.*
>
> —Neuroscientist

Participants also referred to a feeling of *security* that is generated by the acceptance received from group members. Being heard and respected means that they are accepted and can be *free* to be as they are. Recognizing differences within the group and welcoming them is part of this process. People do not want to be rejected.

> *[Belonging] is feeling you can be yourself, and you are loved, welcomed.*
>
> —Personal Stylist, Fashion and Beauty Industry

Having stable social relationships and being part of a group where they feel loved, safe, and accepted generates happiness and better health and acts as a source of resilience, solidarity, and loyalty. Group members are a *personal resource* in times of stress.

> *A sense of belonging to a greater community improves your motivation, health, and happiness. When you see your connection to others, you know that all people struggle and have difficult times. You are not alone. There is comfort in that knowledge.*
>
> —HR VP, Airline Industry

There are multiple groups in which a sense of belonging can be developed; participants mention family, school, the circle of friends, workplace, church, and real or virtual communities, including on social media.

There are some special connotations associated with a sense of belonging in the workplace. When the participants referred to the sense of belonging in an organization, some highlighted that a friendly relationship with their co-workers is a more significant motivator than working conditions, money, and work itself.

Management, working conditions, environment, remuneration, organization; none of them really give employees satisfaction like the statement, 'I have a good friend at work' gives satisfaction.
—Audit Partner, Law Sector

There is an affective component to the sense of belonging in an organization. Having bad social relationships at work, or not having friends, becomes a source of unhappiness and hurts both mental and physical health.

Not having good relations with colleagues decreases an employee's sense of happiness, and it can spoil everything.
—Project Manager, Real Estate

Sharing personal experiences at work helps build empathy between individuals. Some participants described the satisfaction they felt when co-workers were interested in knowing about the well-being of their families. Some also noted how friendly relationships in the workplace were beneficial to their personal lives.

Good relationships in the workplace also motivate and create a sense of security. When individuals feel that they will have support from their co-workers, it encourages them to speak up and share their ideas.

Participants indicated that a vital element for individuals to feel included and accepted in the workplace is recognition associated with the role they have in the organization.

What makes me feel like I'm part of the team is when I'm doing a treatment on a patient and the next day the colleagues tell me that my protocol worked well, healing or whatever; I'm satisfied. It's the fact that my work is valued, the recognition I get. That increases my sense of belonging.
—University Philosophy Professor, Education

CHAPTER 5

The Illusion of Inclusion

We all want to merge and pair, to submerge this lonely 'I' into 'WE'
—Irvin Yalom

In *The Value of Belonging at Work*[1], the authors showed that belonging is a close cousin to many related experiences: mattering, identification, and social connection. The unifying thread across these themes is that they all revolve around the sense of being accepted and included by those around you. They set out to study how that develops—or does not—in the workplace, what it means for employees and organizations, and whether it is possible to turn a bad situation around.

Organizations are being called out on their belonging and inclusion practices. They are being hard-pressed to pursue a culture where everyone feels safe and included. It appears, nevertheless, that organizational approaches are generating a culture of belonging concentrating on awareness-raising and endeavoring to change individual behavior, but we need and we see actions that are targeted at a systemic level.

The Business Case for Belonging

Indeed, a report published by Center Talent Innovation examined a questionnaire of 3,711 college-educated professionals and discovered employees with a greater sense of belonging are more inclined to be engaged, stay at their company for more than two years and recommend it to others.

---

[1] The Value of Belonging at Work by Evan W. Carr, Andrew Reece, Gabriella Rosen Kellerman and Alexi Robichaux HBR, December 16, 2019.
Betterup, 2014. The value of belonging at work: New frontiers for inclusion.

Moreover, researchers at BetterUp[2] observed that high belonging was associated with a 56 percent rise in job performance, a 50 percent fall in turnover risk, and a 75 percent decrease in sick days.

Further research suggests that organizations that prioritize belonging and inclusion during the COVID-19 pandemic may emerge better than before. This was highlighted in a published article in May 2020[3]. Indeed, McKinsey showed that inclusion and diversity are a powerful enabler of business performance. In addition, companies whose leaders welcome diverse talents and include multiple perspectives are likely to emerge from the crisis stronger.

Studies by Deloitte, McKinsey, and EY illustrate that there is a business case for ensuring *belonging* in the workplace. Unfortunately, their studies also show that the implementation of the necessary actions does not always follow. Similar research[4] shows how well-managed belonging programs are also an engine of innovation—leading to the sharing of knowledge, new perspectives, more effective decisions, and alternative paths, leading to better solutions.

Employees with higher workplace belonging showed a 167 percent increase in their employer promoter score (their willingness to recommend their company to others). They also received double the raises, and 18 times more promotions.

—BetterUp

How to encourage leaders to recognize prevailing issues around workforce belonging is an issue currently facing both medium and large companies. This is not just about how to operate at an international level. It is about engaging on a human level to fully benefit from the diverse experience available to develop the company and its employees.

---

[2] BetterUp, 2014. The value of belonging at work New frontiers for inclusion.
[3] The Next Normal: How companies and leaders can reset for growth beyond coronavirus, McKinsey, 2020.
[4] The Next Normal: How companies and leaders can reset for growth beyond coronavirus, McKinsey, 2020.

Language

Social relationships are often based on language. Thus, when English, for example, is the functional or professional language for a group, it is harder for people who are not English speakers to establish relationships (Pullin 2010).

Indeed, talking about personal or more emotional issues and dealing with misunderstandings are areas where the linguistic handicap is felt most (Fredriksson et al. 2007). This is supported by Charles (2008) who indicated the need to reassess linguistic and communicative competence in a world where relationships are central.

Despite these reservations, English has been cited as a language that is quite straightforward and easy for conversations. This is why nonnatives want to talk in English in organizational settings where people speak more frankly and more directly, even if social relationships seem perhaps a little superficial (Kachru 1992).

A coach and consultant in the field of diversity and inclusion, I work with organizations on the topics of collaboration, leadership and self-leadership, team compassion, team care, and team communication. My observation—and this is both case- and research-based—is that organizations still have a long way to go before things are inclusive.

Being part of an organization, a team or a family where we are safe and included gives the feeling that our genuine self is applauded and admired. There is no *persona,* as Carl Jung described, no disguise, no pretext; rather, there is a feeling that we can take our masks off, be ourselves, and feel comfortable contributing. In teams where there is healthy belonging, people are allowed to be themselves, to meet themselves, and have a strong sense of being seen and heard.

Another key is having a deeper understanding of difference. As a coach, I help clients be more conscious of what happens when they work with different teams: What are their red flags? What is their discomfort?

Nonbelonging in Organizations— What Must We Know

Social rejection is at odds with belonging, and the two experiences are inversely related. We have come to understand that social pain caused by ostracism can create a response in our neural processing that is not so different from that caused by physical pain. Even just observing the social anxiety of others can give us painful feelings. When we talk about feeling heartbroken or shattered following a fallout with a friend or social group, we use words that best describe our feelings at that given time. Neuroscientists[5] now have research to support the notion that physical and social pain are not that different from one another.

Yet, belonging is not new; the feeling of being appreciated, respected, and valued has been discussed by psychologists and philosophers for centuries.

But, what makes belonging so imperative and at times so elusive? And, even though it has been shown that there is a positive association between belonging and organizational achievement, why do organizations and leaders continue to battle to create an authentic corporate culture?

And, why do so many organizations give the topic lip service rather than sincerely viewing it as a competitive advantage?

Deloittes work on inclusion in the workplace, "embracing all people, making all people feel valued and feel they belong in their organization," found that millennials view diversity more in terms of cognitive diversity and the range of perspectives that individuals bring, rather than just according to gender, race, and ethnicity. It is also a key factor for millennial decision making about employment. Indeed, the importance of inclusivity for attracting and retaining good employees was clear, *with 80 percent of the respondents saying that inclusion is an important factor in their own decisions about selecting an employer;* 39 percent said they would leave their current employer for a more inclusive one—and 30 percent of the millennials said they had already done so. In addition, 71 percent said that they would rather work for an organization that had inconsistent policies, but demonstrated inclusive behaviors than for one that had wonderful programs and policies that were not translated into behaviors.

---

[5] Race in the workplace: The McGregor-Smith review, 2015.
(Dr. Kelly-Ann Allen MAPS, Psy InPsych, 2019 | Vol 41 June | Issue 3, Making sense of belonging APS.)

A World Economic Forum[6] paper (June 2020) points to the need for companies to integrate diversity, equity, and inclusion into their plans for adopting the Fourth Industrial Revolution and points to the moral, legal, and economic imperatives for doing so. The economic imperatives quoted in this report match some of those given previously and add a 30 percent greater ability of diverse teams to spot and reduce business risks.

Nonbelonging, the Impact on Our Health

The relationship between stress and disease has been well documented by Hungarian-born Canadian physician Gabor Maté[7], an expert in the field of stress, addiction, and childhood development. Indeed, numerous studies have shown that a period of isolation can have deleterious effects on our psyche and morale. A lack of social connectedness when we are alone can have very real somatic and psychological consequences, including withdrawal, depressed mood, generalized anxiety, ruminations, and hostile reactions.

Isolation, loneliness, withdrawal, being alone are terms used to describe situations that may be chosen or experienced by employees and which cover very different realities. Sometimes, these states come with severe consequences for health. Although this phenomenon has been highlighted by many researchers, it remains a serious problem, with more and more employees feeling isolated and lonely. This is true across countries and even when economic circumstances are satisfactory. Indeed, this feeling of loneliness does not seem to be compensated for, despite the increasing use of information and communication technologies. HR and organization heads need to be particularly vigilant for their teams and their people when it comes to the development of new ways of organizing work, such as remote work.

Further support by Snyder-Mackler et al[8] in 2020 showed the importance of connectedness for well-being and endurance in humans

---

[6] Diversity, Equity and Inclusion 4.0: A toolkit for leaders to accelerate social progress in the future of work, World Economic Forum, June 2020.

[7] Dr. Gabor Maté on the Stress-Disease Connection, Addiction and the Destruction of American Childhood, December 25, 2012.

[8] Social determinants of health and survival in humans and other animals Snyder-Mackler1,2,3,4, Joseph Robert Burger1,5,6,7, Lauren*.

and other highly social mammals. The results were clear: *social adversity, and especially isolation, negatively affects health and can shorten lifespan.* In fact, in animal studies, responses to social adversity are detectable at a molecular level. In humans, social adversity was shown to predict "increased mortality risk from almost all major causes of death."

A distinction must be made between *isolation,* as being physically alone, and *loneliness,* which is a negative emotion due to the failure to have satisfying relationships with others. While isolation is the actual state of having no one around, loneliness can be experienced amid a crowd. Being alone, especially if it is our choice, can be a positive experience; indeed, seclusion is another term that can have positive connotations of privacy and retreat.

However, it is important to note that historically, isolation has been synonymous with abuse and punishment for human beings. Thus, to be isolated is to be out of the group and can be experienced as a form of social rejection. Feeling isolated implies that we are experiencing unhappiness linked to our inability to connect with others. And, it is when being alone is experienced as unhappiness and loneliness that it becomes problematic.

The World Health Organization now lists *social support networks* as a determinant of health.

A sense of not belonging is fueling what amounts to a public health epidemic of lack of motivation and meaning and a fear of speaking up. On the physical side, participants in my research noted an increase in anxiety as well as reduced immune function. My findings underline something that many people have felt for some time: we have become less connected with our fellow citizens.

Our society is more divided than many of us would like. It seemed evident that loneliness was a characteristic of the professional participants I interviewed. The nature of some professions is that they are conducted by individuals on their own or by a few individuals choosing to work together. In some cases, professionals have worked in bigger organizations and then choose to work on their own. It is normal to feel lonely when you used to be in business with all that it entails, and you start working on your own. And, it is usual to look for partners with complementary profiles to your own to develop a business or a project. However, complementarity can produce a disparity of points of view and actions taken. Associates may contribute differently by devoting more or less time to the collective project or by developing distinct tasks. The fact that they provide in different ways can convey a sense of imbalance and encourage misunderstandings. Disparity generally generates misunderstanding and favors the emergence of feelings of loneliness.

Impact of Isolation

When one feels alone in the world, stress hormones rise, inflammation increases in the body, and the immune system weakens. *Loneliness can kill you*[9] would be a suitable slogan, but there are no cigarette package-like health warnings to display it, and we certainly hear less about it than obesity or smoking because it is an invisible epidemic.

We know that a lack of attachments and social rejection are at odds with belonging and are linked to a variety of ill effects on health, adjustment, and well-being. In organizational life, this lack of belonging can have huge ramifications. From lessons in neuroscience and neuropsychology, we have come to recognize that social pain caused by exclusion can create a response in our neural processing not so different from that produced by physical pain (Eisenberger, Lieberman and Williams 2003). Furthermore, EY Belonging Barometer, 2019, had some key findings: diversity and belonging have become workplace expectations, and exclusion is experienced as a form of bullying.

---

[9] Social Determinants of Health: The Solid Facts Edited by Richard Wilkinson and Michael Marmot. Social isolation and loneliness as risk factors for myocardial infarction, stroke and mortality: UK Biobank cohort study of 479 054 men and women.
Christian Hakulinen, Laura Pulkki-Råback, Marianna Virtanen, Markus Jokela, Mika Kivimäki, Marko Elovainio.
The Way We Are Now: New study reveals our couple, family, friendships, sex and work secrets, August 2014.

The brain has evolved to react in predictable ways to both threats in our physical settings and to behaviors that benefit our survival. For example, the amygdala reacts to threatening stimuli such as a threat of pain or an approaching lion. Research by Eisenberger NI, and Cole SW, 2012, suggests that social disconnection may be processed in the brain in the same way as for physical harm. Thus, the amygdala sets off an *alarm system* that activates the same range of neurophysiological processes for physical threat of harm and for perceived social isolation. When this alarm system is activated, the processes that are released can contribute to diseases such as diabetes, aging, and cancer. Just observing the social anxiety of others can give us painful feelings. We even use terms such as *feeling heartbroken* or *feeling shattered* after a fallout with a friend or a social group.

According to John Cacioppo, in a TEDx talk entitled *The lethality of loneliness*, we do not talk about feeling lonely because it is stigmatized.

> We tend to celebrate individual achievement, with success marked by what we do and not how we live or give to others. That means admitting to loneliness is tantamount to admitting supreme human failure—the self is not sufficient. It is the psychological equivalent of being a loser in life, or a weak person.

Scientists consider loneliness even more harmful than obesity or smoking. In 2010, Holt-Lunstad published research revealing that people who had strong social relationships had a 50 percent increased likelihood of survival than those with weaker ties. Being disconnected, on the other hand, posed danger comparable to smoking 15 cigarettes a day, and was more predictive of early death than the effects of air pollution or physical inactivity. She noted that, "Regardless of one's sex, country or culture of origin, age or economic background, social connection is crucial to human development, health and survival. Humans need others to survive."

A 2014 study reported by Relate found that 42 percent of the people had no close friend at work. Isolation in the office is now slowly becoming recognized as problematic. The study of more than 5,000 people lifted the lid on the state of the U.K.'s relationships and found that one in 10—around 4.7 million people have no close friends. As professionals, as leaders, this is crucial information to help us appreciate how our attitudes affect our colleagues.

See it. Say it. Sorted.

In 2016, I was traveling from Geneva to London for work. I stopped at London's Waterloo Station to take an intercity train. While I was desperately trying to figure out my next departure time, I heard an announcement; it was a new nationwide campaign to encourage train passengers and station visitors to report any unusual items or activity: "See it. Speak it. Sorted." The campaign was designed to raise awareness of the vital role the public can play in keeping themselves and others safe.

This left me thinking about the whole discussion around connecting in the workplace, often across time zones, across nations, and across different communication styles. What if we did more of "See it. Say it. Sorted."? What if we were not afraid to report anything that felt out of place? What if we spoke up when we saw bias or lack of respect? Could this help to keep all parties safe?

Silence gives consent to discriminating practice, and we are all implicated, no one is exempt. So, unless we all commit to *See it. Speak it. Sorted.* We will continue to perpetuate this unwelcome conduct.

The "See it. Say it. Sorted" model allows leaders to notice what is going on with their teams, talk about it, and sort it out together.

We are social animals. We learn from others by watching them, observing them, and learning from them. So, it takes just one person who dares to speak up to break the pattern.

Reflective exercises
- **See it, say it, sorted.**

See it. You observe something that you do not understand or as unsuitable behavior.

Say it. Do this always with kind intention and ask open-ended questions.

Sort it. Together work toward a mutual understanding. Have a constructive dialogue.

- **Listen**

Listening goes far beyond your natural hearing process. It means paying attention to the what's behind the words that are being spoken with the intention of understanding the other person.

- Do not just think about what the person is saying, but also think about the questions being asked.
- When the other person is talking, offer no justification, explanation, or defense, even if you disagree.
- Mirror and reflect back what has been said to you by paraphrasing. "What I'm hearing is …" and "Sounds like you are saying …" are great phrases to use.
- Enquire and ask open questions to clarify certain points.
- Summarize the person's comments regularly.
- Choose your words.
- Use open questions starting with *when, how, what,* and *who.*
- Comment only on what you observe.
- Keep feedback objective. Keep it simple.

Postreflection
- What worked? What did not work?

Findings and Quotes From my Research

The Impact of the Sense of Nonbelonging

When individuals feel that they do not fit into a group or organization, the effects can be far-reaching. Some participants referred to studies that show that not belonging can generate the same sensation as physical pain. They warn that, when an organization makes no effort to create a workplace focused on the emotions of its employees, the result may be unhappiness, a deterioration in physical and mental health, decreased motivation and productivity, increased absenteeism, and poor retention of talent. All of this will result in an economic cost to the organization.

Unhappiness

According to the participants, loneliness, isolation, and social exclusion in the organization cause unhappiness. This can also occur when there is no integration process in the case of new employees.

I was new to the company, and there was no effective integration pro-cess. I felt very isolated and lonely. Looking back, I could have changed the team culture, but I felt outnumbered.

—Professor, Executive Education

Management plays a determining role. Some participants attributed their unhappiness to the poor support and recognition they received from management.

My manager did not feel that I was good enough and I felt really rejected, excluded, and this was difficult to live through especially when you put all your heart ... this feeling of rejection was not good ...

—Head of Funds, Private Equity

I worked in an organization where I was hired by, but had no support at all from my direct manager, and I felt like I was really kind of left like the dogs and my peers really took advantage of the situation ... I had no support, I was alone. ... I became very nervous and very anxious and very self-doubting of myself.

—Lead Broadcaster, Broadcasting

Impact of Nonbelonging Mental and Physical Health

Those who have felt a lack of belonging in an organization and little sup-port from management to deal with it affirmed that this affected their sleep, they had low energy, they were emotionally and mentally tired, they became nervous and anxious.

I know it's impacting my department and some of my people in my teams are really suffering from feeling really battered, emotionally tired, not recognized, not validated, and it's causing them much stress.

Consultant, Financial Consulting

The anxiety described by one of the participants was related to the fear he felt to ask for clarification on assigned activities. He did not feel safe speaking. One participant, who did dare to speak, said that when his interventions were ignored, this affected his well-being.

Participants who felt excluded, disconnected from co-workers, or treated with indifference described how they began to suffer from a variety of illnesses, including stomach pain, thyroid problems, and even facial paralysis. Depression was common. Self-esteem was affected, as they began to doubt their own effectiveness at work. One talked about being furious when in the workplace and another about being overwhelmed by emotions.

> *I remember feeling sick to the stomach about going to work, so I often took time off work because I was feeling physically ill my anxiety was so bad. And even when I was at work, I was paranoid. I'm thinking 'Oh God, what's the day going to bring?' It's had a long-lasting impact on my career and mental health. It had a massive impact on my self-esteem and self-worth because I started to question myself.*
>
> —VP Operations, Medical

> *I began to feel irritable at home as a consequence of the stressful situation at work. I began questioning the purpose of my role at work and home, and feelings of worthlessness, despair and depression began to surface. I did not expect to be so overwhelmed with the emotional stress that this brought me.*
>
> —Innovation Department, Banking Industry

Some turned to friends and family for relief. Others needed to go to mental health professionals. Unfortunately, for some, the stress generated by feeling that their work was not recognized or valued sometimes spilled over into irritability that they expressed at home.

CHAPTER 6

Self-Actualizing Leaders

We tend to celebrate individual achievement, with success marked by what we do and not how we live or give to others. That means admitting to loneliness is tantamount to admitting supreme human failure—the self is not sufficient. It is the psychological equivalent of being a loser in life, or a weak person.

—John Cacioppo

Organizations need a roadmap for developing competent leaders, whether they are aspiring to achieve sustainable competitive advantage in today's global economy or to create a workplace where everyone's talents can shine. To feel human, active, and full of life includes the ability to help and lead others to avoid the obstacles that interfere in their lives to realize their full potential. Anything is achievable when we belong, especially when human potential is uninhibited.

There are countless definitions of leadership, and there are many expectations of leaders in organizations. Bass (1990) defines leaders as *agents of change*; persons whose actions affect other people more than other people's actions affect them. Leadership is demonstrated when one member of the group (and it can be any member) brings about a change in motivation or competency of others in the group.

Avolio et al (2004) bring our attention to *authenticity* in leaders. These are leaders who are profoundly aware of how they think and behave; they are concerned with their own and others' values, moral perspectives, knowledge, and strengths; they are aware of the context in which they operate; they are confident, hopeful, optimistic, resilient, and of high moral character. Peter Salovey and John Mayers (1997) define leadership in terms of *emotional intelligence*. These leaders give attention to using emotions in positive and productive ways.

Jones et al also examined the importance of *psychological contracts* in the workplace in their paper titled, *Leadership: Untapping, the Secret to Regional Wellbeing, Belonging and Resilience*. Psychological contracts are the unwritten set of expectations, beliefs, and obligations that exist between employees and their managers. These expectations include the need to be valued and respected and regarded as important to the organization. It can be demonstrated in conversations, body language, voice tone. The researchers found that any violations of the psychological agreement could prove damaging to the welfare of the individual, the organization, and the wider community. Conversely, when the contract is met, the outcomes are well-being, resilience, and belonging.

Leadership That Gets Outcomes

Naturally, one cannot be a leader without followers. You do not stay a trusted team leader for long if team members do not believe in you. Jim Collins (researcher and author of what makes great companies tick), in *Good to Great*, encourages leaders to strive to become a Level 5 leader.

> Level 5 leaders channel their ego needs away from themselves and into the larger goal of building a great company. It's not that Level 5 leaders have no ego or self-interest. Indeed, they are incredibly ambitious—but their ambition is first and foremost for the institution, not themselves.

(Jim Collins and Good to Great 2001) But, how does a leader achieve this? Part of the answer lies in understanding the needs of human beings and how they strive to meet those needs.

Self-actualization is the need to become what one has the potential to be. It has its roots in the theories put forward by Abraham Maslow.

> *What a man can be, he must be. This need we call self-actualization.*
> Abraham Maslow

According to Maslow, once people have been able to meet their basic needs—physiological, security, love and belonging, respect, and esteem—they can then focus on their growth needs, and specifically on self-actualizing. He noted that this is very much an internal need. It is not focused on external gain or concern about what others might say.

Self-actualization refers to the natural process of development that drives us to become fully human, fully alive. It is the need to become all that we can become, to progress beyond inferior, purely instrumental needs, to satisfy our obligation to be the noblest, to discover and express our unique talents and abilities. It is to experience high points in our lives, those moments when we feel we are in the *zone* and give the best of ourselves. It is to live for our higher needs for beauty, order, truth, love, expression, contribution, and excellence.

The psychology of self-actualization focuses on the good side of human nature. It helps people move from a state where they are just *okay* to a life where they become the best version of themselves. It is a philosophy that aims to generate human excellence and describes how to attain real human potential.

What are the elements of self-actualizing?

1. *Becoming all that you can be.*
2. *Developing as a human being to become fully functional.*
3. *Experiencing one's humanity and full individuality.*
4. *Having synergy between meaning and performance.*

Some people find it more challenging to actualize themselves than others. The need for security may hinder a person's actualization. The person may have learned to become not what he or she is, but rather what others want him or her to be. Most of the time, this goes against their actualization.

When all is said and done, self-actualization is a personal responsibility to have the courage to be who you are and to step out from yourself.

Self-Actualizing Leadership

The first step to actualize yourself is by developing your potential through whatever you do every day. This builds your own happiness. But, people do not develop talents on their own or use them only for their own benefit. When your talents are put to use in the service of others, you share your happiness with others and share in their happiness too.

Perhaps, this is what is meant by unleashing your potential. As a leader, it has particular implications for all of those whom you touch, either directly or indirectly. And, it also has implications for human capital and talent. What potential is latent, is hidden, and how do we invoke and release it?

The intensity of the need to actualize yourself is related to your own inner strength. It is a process of fulfillment that spreads out over the whole of life. It is fostered by your self-awareness, your individual inner faculties, and by the environment in which you evolve.

This brings us back again to Maslow's hierarchy of needs. Self-actualization can be held back by nonachievement of the lower level, or more, basic needs. One of these is a sense of belonging, and others are esteem and respect.

Thus, it becomes part of the responsibility of leaders and organizations to provide the environment that will foster the achievement of these needs. In work settings, an attitude of openness and acceptance seems to be an effective way of overcoming the obstacles that hinder the process of self-realization. Acceptance itself becomes part of actualizing oneself.

> My research participants discussed how much time and money organizations invest to attract new talent; so, absenteeism and resignations generate an additional cost. This is one more reason to invest in a culture of belonging.

Maslow, as we have shown, was interested in individuals engaged in the process of realization of potential. He describes them as freer, more spontaneous, more creative than the average person, both empathetic and self-confident. Maslow gave the name of "the self-actualizers," to those people who are the best and brightest, the most productive, the healthiest, who made the most significant difference in the world, who contributed the most to its development, and who lived life as a sequence of optimal experiences.

They reach a kind of fulfillment through art, philosophy, wisdom, spirituality, or ethics. How many are there? He believed about 2 percent of the population at most. But, this *superior* humanity (Maslow uses this word) is not closed. We can model the lifestyle of those who are self-actualized and teach these models of excellence. The self-actualizers are not some kind of elite, we can all self-actualize.

In his book *Transcendence*, Scott Kauffman notes that the characteristics of self-actualizing people are even more relevant today than when they were first proposed nearly 70 years ago. Kaufmann stipulates:

we live in times of increasing divides, selfish concerns, and individualistic pursuits of power and I fear Maslow's conceptualization of self-actualization and the vision of humanity that was prevalent among the humanistic psychologists of the 60 and 70s has been lost in this generation.

However, Kauffman believes that Maslow was very mistaken in thinking that self-actualization was notably tenuous in the population, especially as he argued it was unattainable among young people. Kauffman found through his research that self-actualization scores corresponded to a normal distribution, much the same as IQ or height. What is more, self-actualization is *not* correlated with age, education, race, ethnicity, college grade point average (GPA), or childhood income. Besides, there were no gender differences found in self-actualization.

While there are undoubtedly environmental barriers to self-actualization, some environments can help bring out the best (or the worst) in us. He found no evidence that the characteristics of self-actualization are limited to a particular swath of humanity.

Self-actualizing leadership is an approach that allows us to live fully and humanely. It focuses on a way of leading meaningfully and joyfully. Fundamental to self-actualizing leadership is the leader's recognition of the need for his or her own actualization. It is not enough to encourage the development of others. Self-development and self-growth are the requirements for any form of legitimate leadership.

However, as the models described earlier show, there are high expectations for leader behavior. Employees are looking for leaders who become role models for personal growth, authenticity, emotional intelligence, and the ability to uphold unwritten contracts of support. They expect them to provide the environment that will allow the organization itself and everyone in it to thrive.

A leader's authority depends on being perceived as a person of integrity. Leaders who act hypocritically undermine their positions. (Perhaps, a reminder to leaders that they cannot pretend to do the right things comes from the comments from the participants in my research. Please see the end of this chapter for quotes).

As a result, reflection and practices which are emerging for leadership development can be classified into three families: in addition to activities of analytical understanding of the system, attention is also being given to tasks of emotional intelligence and practices of mindfulness.

Whether we are thinking of an environment, a workplace, or a community organization, it is the people with authority who should make sure that people feel welcomed, included, and accepted. Sometimes, I see leaders who are able to generate calm rather than anxiety. They encourage others to speak up, and they have respect for people. They have no hidden agendas. They are not interested in taking over the space. They are the guides on the side and not the sages on the stage. I have such admiration when I come across leaders like these, because they know that it is their responsibility to "Keep it Real. Keep it Relevant. Keep it Safe."

Checklist of What Self-Actualizing Leaders Do

1. They are generous and genuine when they give feedback and avoid empty compliments.
2. They have accurate understanding for people being fully seen and understood and know that it is as vital as water and food.
3. They see belonging as a team sport. They reflect on how they can create more belonging, with the hope that it then trickles down to the rest of the team.
4. They share their errors and acknowledge mistakes. They use their feelings as data points.
5. Self-disclosure is essential; no one gains without disclosure.

6. They have acquired *rabbit ears*, picking up that every person in the team responds differently to an identical stimulus. Each has a unique inner understanding of the subject at hand, and it may have a different significance to each of them.

7. They give feedback gently, focusing on feelings and facts.

8. They help people assume responsibility. If they see their problems as outside of themselves, they help them adapt or attain level-headedness, or teach them to be more effective at altering their environment.

9. When in doubt, they go inside and look inward and find understanding.

Reflective Exercise

Self-Actualizing Leadership Assessment

1. How would you describe your professional and personal self?
2. Where do you feel more authentic?
3. What tensions can you identify between these different identities?
4. Which behaviors would you like to do more of?
5. Which behaviors would you like to do less off?
6. How could you improve to become a more *self-actualizing leader*?

Findings and Quotes From My Research

Loss of Motivation and Productivity

Motivation and performance of employees are clearly negatively impacted by the unhappiness, stress, low self-esteem, and physical discomfort that were described by participants.

> *I felt a withdrawal that included a diminished motivation, (less) alliance to peer groups and thoughts of leaving the organization. Not to mention the feeling of insecurity, which hinders productivity gains.*
> —Finance Head, Gaming Industry

There is a sense of feeling isolated, indifferent and demotivated.

—Project Manager, Green Energy

Lack of connection with company values negatively impacts employees' commitment to the organization's goals and vision.

I just played the game, but I was sneaky and did not fully trust, share or commit.

—Deputy Head, Education

When you don't have pride in working for your company, this is one of the main factors that guarantees unhappiness, disengagement and disconnection at work.

—Chief of Staff, International Organization

Absenteeism and Loss of Talent

When the lack of belonging in the organization causes unhappiness, physical pain, or more severe illnesses, some individuals start to take days off, while others decide to leave.

The absence of psychological safety made me so uncomfortable. It affected my sleep and my energy. I had to leave because it was impacting my health.

—Head of F&B, Hospitality

Other participants focused their attention on the inconsistency between the values of the company and the values of the employees as a fundamental cause of loss of talent.

The major reason why I changed my company was because it was important to feel a sense of belonging and I need to be aligned with the company values. It really comes down to a question of fit and if that fit gives you a sense of belonging.

—Chief Diversity Officer, FMCG

It is fundamental that a company that wishes to avoid turnover and high absenteeism must have a strong and inspiring culture that

*conveys values that connect with the employee who represents it. The
employee must feel that he or she is part of something bigger than
himself or herself and that he or she is honored to be its spokesperson.*

—Relationship Manager, Wealth Management

Lack of recognition also drives individuals to leave organizations. Not
being appreciated for the work that they do or the effort that they invest
generates unhappiness and affects employee well-being. Many opt to
move to another organization that does offer recognition.

*I felt totally denied of recognition; my integrity was violated.
I felt very sad, maybe even depressed, so I [had] no choice. I left the
organization.*

—Senior Director, Finance

*If you don't have a sense of belonging to the company you work for,
to whom you give a lot of hours a week, for whom you perform, for
whom you get up every morning, sooner or later you will have the
desire to go elsewhere because you will be driven by the desire to belong
to something more powerful.*

—Philosophy Professor, Executive Education

Two participants discussed how much time and money organizations
invest to attract new talent; so, absenteeism and resignations generate an
additional cost. This is one more reason to invest in a culture of belonging.

CHAPTER 7

The Power of Allies

No Man is an Island

—John Dunne

An ally is any person who actively encourages and seeks to promote the culture of belonging in deliberate, emphatic, and purposeful efforts that benefits everyone as a whole. Everyone can be an ally, a powerful lever. Naturally, leaders are the best situated to create belonging in their teams, but ultimately, it is we all who are accountable.

Bea Young[1], a pioneer in the field of educational equity, discusses the role of allies as being paramount in a structure.

The role of the ally is not to rescue, not to save, but to help work it out instead of acting out. Allies focus on the here and now, on the individual with the focus on being proactive and not passive.

In the late 1920s, Elton Mayo, a professor at Wharton and Harvard, exhibited that labor efficiency is based primarily on concern for workers, well before objective working conditions. Almost a 100 years later, compassion is still a noble virtue in corporate life.

Being able to express one's emotions and hear those of others is one of the conditions for creative cooperation. Working together toward a common goal allows teams to move forward, enriched by the exchanges and contributions of each other.

But, what is compassion? According to the Buddhist tradition, it is defined as the desire to bring an end to the sufferings of others and their causes. It is an altruistic act of kindness. Based on the principle

---

[1] Matthieu Ricard is a well-known French writer, photographer, translator, and Buddhist monk.

of interdependence, that is, the fact that we are all connected to others, compassion is meant to be the binding agent that helps us to enter into harmonious relationships first with ourselves and then with others.

Empathy and Mirror Neurons

Empathy is recognizing, understanding, and appreciating how other people feel. Empathy involves being able to articulate your understanding of another's perspective and behaving in a way that respects the feelings of others.

Dan Batson in his book, *The Social Neuroscience of Empathy*, explores eight ways the word and concept of empathy are used.

1. Knowing another person's internal state, including thoughts and feelings.
2. Adopting the posture or matching the neural responses of an observed other.
3. Coming to feel as another person feels.
4. Intuiting or projecting oneself into another's situation.
5. Imagining how another is thinking and feeling.
6. Imagining how one would think and feel in the other's place.
7. Feeling distressed at witnessing another person's suffering.
8. Feeling for another person who is suffering.

Some researchers believe that the cornerstone of human empathy is in our *mirror neurons*. These are neurons in the frontal lobes of the brain. Research shows that certain neurons fire up when we undertake certain activities—and that they also fire when we are watching someone else undertaking the same activity. This includes a subset of these neurons that respond to another person's pain and emotions.

A Ted Talk by Neurologist VS Ramachandran suggested that all that is separating you from the other person is your skin. Remove the skin, and you will experience that person's touch in your mind. The mirror neuron system allows you to rethink specific issues such as consciousness, representation of self, what separates you from other human beings, what enables you to empathize with other human beings, and even the emergence of culture and civilization, which is unique to human beings.

Perhaps mirror neurons explain the skills involved in creating rapport. One reliable method to increase rapport, which I encourage my clients to use, is to mirror posture, gestures, facial expressions, and even breathing of those we wish to connect with. Natural communication is improved as both verbal and nonverbal characteristics are involved.

Another skill to improve empathy is to take on the role of an observer, detached and balanced, looking at a situation as if you were not a part of it. This perceptual position as an external, impartial observer, dissociated emotionally and detached from the situation, will enable you to have a balanced approach, especially in emotionally charged cases.

Of course, if you are in fact involved in the interaction, this means that you are also being observed from a distance. You step back and *watch yourself*—it is like seeing the situation on a movie screen.

While empathy functions as a simple mirror of other people's emotions, compassion infers a feeling of caring, with a willingness to help the person who is suffering.

We must review how we treat each other, how we see each other. As micro aggressions and behaviors may seem harmless, but each one has a massive impact.

> Microaggressions are everyday actions and behaviors that have harmful effects on marginalized groups. Unlike other forms of discrimination, the perpetrator of microaggression may or may not be aware of the harmful effects of their behavior.

I want us all to hold a mirror up to ourselves, and when I did it, I did not like what I saw. This could be an effective measure in appreciating that our actions and comments, however small, have influence and impact. It is our responsibility to be accountable. And, not just because of the impact it has on performance and business objectives, but because it is the right thing to do.

Consequently, the ultimate goal of a compassionate culture is creating a community that has a sense of belonging, a shared identity, shared values and goals. Subsequently, we are together both because we are doing something together, but also because of who we are.

In his book *The Healing Power of Human Connection in a Sometimes-Lonely World*, Vivek Murthy shows that loneliness may have become a public health issue, can be harmful, and is on the rise today. *The stigma of feeling lonely, he witnessed was rampant, but rarely discussed openly.*

However, if we are really concerned about the sufferings or misfortunes of others, we can do something about it. If we create better connections with our friends and our communities, we can lead healthier lives and help our friends be healthier too.

A sense of belonging, he argues, is not equivalent to believing you are alike to everyone else. Our appetite to assimilate frequently forces us to suppress who we are.

Further, evidence for more compassion is backed by renowned Buddhist monk[2] Matthieu Ricard, the practice of mindfulness is still too often presented to managers as a tool to reduce stress, improve concentration, and develop concentration. Of course, these benefits are proven, but according to Ricard, several essential dimensions are just as rich for the company and for all who work in the organization. Among these is better decision making and the ability to take better consideration of colleagues and collaborators in a caring way. This last dimension, in particular, is crucial to promote harmony at work and the fulfillment of each individual. Belonging is when you feel safe and appreciated for incorporating what makes you different, your uniqueness. We feel a sense of belonging when a colleague does not agree with our idea solely on the fact that it is not the most suitable option, and not because of anything amiss with us. The evidence is clear—the most powerful force for belonging is care, empathy, respect, and connection.

It seems that it is enough to develop a sense of belonging, and motivation and commitment are almost guaranteed to follow. Nonetheless, the feeling of belonging is not permanent; it can fluctuate according to situations that only the organization can influence.

Thus, maintaining belonging is an ongoing effort on the part of the authority figures in the organization.

A Real-Life Case Study of a Compassionate Community

Snuggled in a leafy suburb of Geneva, Switzerland, La Maison de Tara offers an alternative to hospitalization for people nearing the end of their lives.

---

[2] Matthieu Ricard https://matthieuricard.org/en/

It is for those who are unable to stay at home but wish to spend their final days in a nonmedicalized atmosphere surrounded by warmth, care and tenderness it is a home away from home. It offers to any person, young or old, who is seriously ill, a place to stay and be cared for in a family atmosphere.

I am very proud to say that I am part of the volunteer family at La Maison de Tara. I was welcomed and trusted to be part of the family right from the very beginning.

The founder, Anne-Marie Struijk, wanted to set up a loving space where people could die within a community and with love and care. The eloquent words of Dame Cecily Saunders, U.K. founder of the hospice movement and modern palliative care, summarizes the philosophy of Tara: *"You matter because you are you, and you matter to the end of your life. We will do all we can not only to help you die peacefully but also to live until you die."*

The house is managed by a team of two, the founder and Sabine Murbach, a Foundation Trustee. They also direct and coordinate the activities of the salaried staff and volunteer groups who contribute to our work.

Organogram of La Maison de Tara

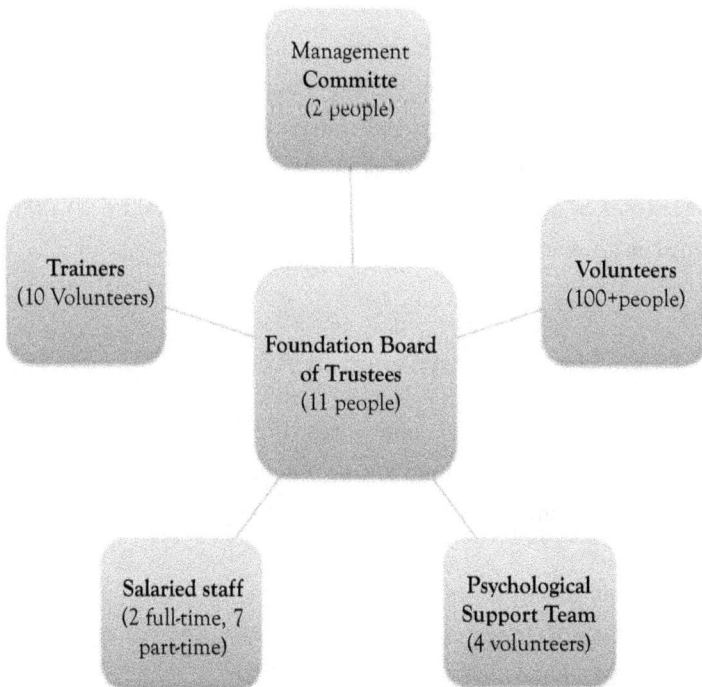

Management Committe (2 people)

Trainers (10 Volunteers)

Volunteers (100+people)

Foundation Board of Trustees (11 people)

Salaried staff (2 full-time, 7 part-time)

Psychological Support Team (4 volunteers)

One of their primary roles is to guide, train, and lead a team of volunteers. All volunteers get over 100 hours of training in basic knowledge of palliative care, practical know-how, and *how to be* with themselves, with residents and their families. Training is given by both in-house and external people with deep experience of palliative care.

The volunteers belong to various professions, cultures, and contexts and have collectively accumulated multiple life experiences and skills that they bring to the effective functioning of La Maison de Tara. At present, they number more than 100 volunteers, representing over 15 different nationalities and speaking a wide variety of languages.

There are regular cycles of training, which enable new volunteers to join the team. Increasingly, in our society, many people do not have a family or social network that is sufficiently wide to offer a sense of community care. In addition, a sense of loss may generate powerful emotions, which may be challenging to cope with for the patient, the family, and close friends. Caring for people at the end of their lives might be the ultimate demonstration of compassion. However, one thing that touched me when I started volunteering was the importance and care placed also on the team of volunteers.

Except despite all my leadership coaching experience and high-performing teams, I still could not figure out one burning question: how did the volunteers who come together in groups of four, daily, alternating three shifts a day, seven days a week, work so well together?

Hence, I began to observe and take mental notes, and this is what I learned as I observed them.

Compassion in Action

1. They work toward the same vision. The *triumphs* are the result of teamwork, so it is essential to accept it and share it.
2. Their roles and responsibilities are clearly defined, and expectations are clarified.
3. They build on people's strengths.
4. They encourage opportunities to share our concerns and opinions even if we know that not everyone will agree.

5. They recognize that an accumulation of frustration can prolong conflicts and feelings of resentment toward our colleagues, the battle becomes magnified, and there is a reduction in performance.

6. They listen to each other with their hearts, and we take the time to hear each other. There are no silly questions; there are no stupid ideas; all uncertainties and all thoughts are equal.

7. They do not judge, and we do not criticize each other under any circumstances. We avoid saying, "You should have done it this way."

8. They acknowledge the joint work that has been done by one and all.

9. There is always a check in and *check out* where they evaluate progress and congratulate each other on a job well done.

These sound practices are not rules, and therefore, they are not absolute. You are free to apply them as they are, to adapt them, to draw inspiration from them. And, if belonging is what all employees desire in the workplace, how can we create the experience of true belonging? My experience at La Maison de Tara has taught me a great deal about how this is done. Much of it is about *checking in* with people to make sure that they do not *check out*. *Checking in* can be seen as a form of compassion—it says that you care about what is happening to the other.

Organizational life is, by nature, anxiety-producing and stress-generating. Each of us has to face our problems, and it is often difficult to find the time and energy to help our colleagues face theirs. But, it all becomes more manageable once we realize that care and empathy can make people around us feel more at ease with the obstacles they face.

Ultimately, what allows the team to create a real cohesion and to move forward together toward a common goal is that we show love and compassion for ourselves first and foremost, and then for our colleagues. I think that is fundamental, I encourage you to show loving kindness to yourselves first and foremost.

Everyone has the potential to be an ally. Allies make a collective effort to support.

Being an ally is not only hard work, but also heart work. It is necessary to bring your whole self to work, to fully apply yourself, to take personal responsibility, exceed your objectives and your own expectations. This is how you can inspire yourself and others. This is how you can move the needle and create a true culture of belonging.

Lessons from a High-Performing Compassionate Team
How is this Achieved?

- Firstly, we are all, each one of us, going to have to learn how to listen and be more curious. I often tell my clients that the three most powerful words in business are, "Tell me more."

The three most important words in business. Every time you want to speak, ask a question, and if you cannot think of a question, these three little words have immense power and data for you to see what is going on in your team.

- Secondly, it is leaders who need to model this behavior and pay attention to any tension in the team. This is a powerful way to build team cultures where people feel they belong—and this can happen even if they are not physically present.
- Thirdly, if people are not yet sure they belong on the team, how will they possibly be comfortable sharing their innermost thoughts? I found it was necessary to pivot to a slower and steadier approach with new team members.
- Fourthly, it is important to create a support system around learning. Although there may have been a formal training program, the real learning occurs on the job. Once the training session is over, it is imperative to follow up with application, integration, and continued feedback. The action happens outside the classroom. Neither should exist in isolation; the two need to merge into one, in order for it to become part of the organizational values.
- Finally, we need to accept that we are all responsible for building a sense of belonging in the workplace. We all need to *check in* with others.

Findings From My Research

The Positive Effects of the Sense of Belonging in Organizations

Some of the positive outcomes of feeling that you belonged in an organization included happiness, well-being, engagement, motivation, loyalty, productivity, and retention.

Happiness

Individuals feel satisfaction and happiness when there are healthy social relationships with co-workers, they feel part of a team, know that their ideas are heard and respected, that their work is recognized and valued, and believe that they are contributing to a common purpose.

Also, individuals need to know that their work has meaning, and that they are part of something greater than themselves. When employees can identify with the values, vision, and goals of the organization, then they feel happiness.

Well-Being

Participants attributed improved well-being to a sense of belonging. Having friends at work, having shared aspirations and the support of co-workers, being listened to, respected and valued all lead to a sense of belonging and therefore to a sense of well-being. It reflects positively on mental and physical health and is demonstrated in positive emotions, reduced stress and illness, and improved sleep.

Well-being is also reflected in improved self-esteem and occurs in a work environment where employees are accepted as they are and where they can develop their skills.

Engagement

Some participants noted how a sense of belonging increases employees' commitment to the organization. A bond forms between them that goes beyond a contract. When there is a connection with co-workers and with the organization, individuals will take initiatives and improve their performance to help the organization achieve its goals.

Forming bonds with other people generates positive emotions that lead to the desire to collaborate and to work as a team.

Motivation

Motivation levels go up for employees who experience shared interests and goals and who have friendly relationships in the workplace. The feeling of security generated by connections with other co-workers will also motivate them to take risks; they can be more creative and innovative. They will want to do the *best job of their lives.*

Loyalty

Creating a sense of belonging in the organization will help build employee loyalty. Individuals with a high sense of belonging in the organization will tend to speak well about their workplace.

Productivity

For some participants, the sense of belonging in the organization is becoming an *imperative* and a *key element* of success. When the organization and its employees have the same purpose and are oriented to achieve the same goals, productivity increases.

One of the participants described how the ability to think, process information, and develop ideas is related to well-being at work. If well-being is high, the individual becomes more motivated and productive.

This increase in productivity is also related to the collaboration that arises between team members to achieve common goals.

The satisfaction associated with the sense of belonging in the organization will translate into success for the company.

Retention

The chances of employees staying in the company increase once they have a sense of belonging in the organization or have developed a strong and stable relationship with the team. A culture of belonging, thus, helps organizations retain talent.

Joint Benefit

At the end of the day, participants believed that a sense of belonging had benefits for both the individual and the organization.

It seems that it is enough to develop a sense of belonging, and motivation and commitment are almost guaranteed to follow. Nonetheless, the feeling of belonging is not permanent; it can fluctuate according to situations that only the organization can influence. Thus, maintaining it is an ongoing effort on the part of the authority figures in the organization.

Be the Ally to be the Change
- Be ready, emotionally, physically, and psychologically
- Be kind
- Be open
- Be curious
- Be aware of your biases
- Be the change you would like to see

CHAPTER 8

Belonging at a Distance

Belonging will become increasingly relevant in the aftermath of a pandemic, economic disruption and social unrest.

—Lanaya Irvin

Dr. Elke Van Hoof, Professor of Health Psychology and Primary Care Psychology, Vrije Universiteit in Brussels[1], warned in a recent World Economic Forum note that the COVID-19 lockdown was the world's biggest psychological experiment. He predicted "a secondary epidemic of burnouts and stress-related absenteeism" as an outcome of the quarantine.

The new normal has become the catchphrase to describe life after the first shock of the COVID-19 pandemic. But, what does it mean? And, more importantly, what is the next normal, and what are the new possibilities that can emerge?

COVID-19

People have felt a multitude of emotions and a wide variety of feelings during the ongoing COVID-19 crisis. Participants interviewed when they were in lockdown described fear and anxiety, and yet, they also declared a need for more belonging, connectedness, and a call for solidarity and community.

Every person, regardless of color, religion, political belief, or social status, has witnessed daily life torn apart by the COVID-19 virus. However, the virus has also offered some of us the time to take a break, to slow down, to simplify our lives, and to take care of ourselves and our loved

---

[1] The World Economic Forum COVID Action Platform. Lockdown is the world's biggest psychological experiment—and we will pay the price 09 April 2020.

ones. It may also provide the opportunity to build a real community of belonging and inclusive practice and to help each other. The fact that there are billions of people living this same experience will undeniably bring people together, even though it is being managed and dealt with differently from one context to another.

When I interviewed participants during the COVID-19 lockdown, I observed the shift in responses to a greater concern for balance and for our social ties and also to see the important role that organizations play in binding us together. I also witnessed feelings of helplessness and isolation, especially in the face of a changing world and what was perceived to be hyper-control and hyper-power being demonstrated by leaders. Many people were forced to stay at home and not allowed to associate with anyone. Some participants in my research project (mainly ones who lived alone) reported feelings of deep loneliness and the loss of connection with their co-workers. The forced isolation awakened the anguish of a more fundamental isolation for some. In Chapter 4 I referred to the work of Sandstrom and Granovetter and their research on the power of *weak ties* and casual relationships. They showed that people are happier and have more of a sense of belonging if they have extensive connections and groupings with a fairly wide range of people, even if these relationships are relatively casual and superficial. These casual connections are also a source of learning and information.

This made me wonder what the impact was of the removal of many of these casual connections during the time of lockdown—the day-to-day conversations with people in shops, at the gym, at places of worship and at school or with fellow employees who are not members of your own team. Is it possible that people's stark feelings of isolation were as much a result of the loss of these weak ties as they were of the more formal and close ties?

Conversely, it seems also to point to the importance for people to engage in as wide a range of conversations as they can during this time. This would provide stimulation but also, in a time of uncertainty, guidance on how to behave.

Maslow's Hierarchy of Needs in the New Normal

During the period of painful lockdown, I asked questions to a new set of participants in my research. I observed that participants were more reflective in their responses and able to take stock of the past and the uncertain future. There was more talk of balance and our ties. Many more of them talked about family and belonging outside work than those I interviewed before the start of the pandemic. Some participants saw this as a real opportunity to build a different type of organization and society.

But, there were also concerns about how to deal with the anguish of a changing world. There were feelings of helplessness and isolation, together with the stress of not knowing what the future will hold. There was a sense of trepidation about the future. Many were concerned and confused by what was going on in the minds of leaders, who seem concerned only about control and power. Many were pleading for a more peaceful conception of power relations.

Others talked about how the heightened need for emotional resilience might have been underestimated. Working remotely, uncertainty about the future, concerns about illness, and fears about job security increased the need for resilience. Emotional fatigue was particularly common where employees felt that there was not a sense of belonging in their teams.

Stress was a central theme through all my interviews, both before and during COVID-19. Generally, stress is defined as the physical and psychological pressure or strain experienced by an individual in response to events that have taken place. People in my survey experienced different aspects and identified with different definitions. Several participants reported physical and emotional stress experienced as a response to a sense of not belonging. Some participants had been under an enormous amount of personal stress; this, in turn, had a tremendous effect on their interactions and perceptions of any work-related issues. It is perhaps not surprising that stress at work and its effect on well-being is no longer regarded as just a health issue. It also has economic implications, costing organizations millions of dollars due to both absenteeism and presenteeism (being at work, but not fully functioning).

I was struck by the change in the way people were articulating their needs. Before COVID-19, energy was focused on the highest levels of Maslow's pyramid, looking for respect and esteem and self-actualization. And, now? We are rushing down the levels to the ground floor. We are concerned about basic needs. We are suddenly worried about physiological needs such as food and warmth and health. We are particularly worried about security and safety. *Lockdown in a strange way met our need for safety. But, it led to a surge in our need to be with people, to belong, to be loved.*

Belonging, intimacy, and closeness are somewhat artificial in the new normal. All of us are now facing questions we cannot answer; the uncertainty of not knowing is difficult for the soul and the brain. The COVID-19 crisis is disturbing our security, our health, and our links with others.

I have seen so many mentions of *belonging* in books, media, and articles over the past few months. People yearn for it more than ever during this time of social distancing. One thing is sure—we are suffering without access to our communities.

The lockdown also brought out some different aspects of nonbelonging. During the pre-COVID-19 interviews, the discussion was about nonbelonging in organizations. Many participants interviewed during the lockdown were more concerned about not belonging in their communities. The nonbelonging problem was underscored in an article by John Cho[2] in the *Los Angeles Times*:

> Asian Americans are experiencing such a moment right now. The pandemic is reminding us that our belonging is conditional. One moment we are Americans, the next, we are all foreigners, who 'brought' the virus here.

I had hoped when I started undertaking my research and writing this book that I would be able to demonstrate how important belonging was for the workplace. Now, it is even clearer to me that belonging cannot be conditional. Belonging is what makes us feel protected and secure. It has to be guaranteed—in communities, in teams, and in organizational cultures.

Belonging in the New Normal

The world of work responded to this need for safety, community, and belonging through digital communication—and work will probably never be the same again as a result.

---

[2] John Cho Op-Ed: John Cho: Coronavirus Reminds Asian Americans Like Me That Our Belonging Is Conditional Dr Elke Van Hoof Professor. *Health Psychology and Primary Care Psychology*. Vrije Universiteit Brussel.

Some participants discussed the challenge of instilling team spirit from a distance. They perceived the most important thing to do was to remain available to talk to each other as regularly as possible and to maintain some office practices remotely; these do not necessarily have to be related to working activity but to help keep the feeling of belonging.

Seeing colleagues, peers, and leaders—even though it was online—gave participants some reassurance because they all had the same worries, especially in times of isolation.

There is some evidence to show that teams working during the COVID-19 pandemic strengthened bonds and attachment to the group. Online team meetings were reported to be successful—but only if the leaders or team leads displayed emotional intelligence. When leaders took time to show care, by checking in and checking out, asking questions and showing empathy, participants described an elevated sense of engagement, motivation, and belonging.

What was very interesting was how many people mentioned that they were worried about going back to the office.

However, some participants talked about cognitive overload associated with multiple online meetings and the blurring of boundaries between work and private life. In a time of crisis, they also had to support their own families and friends. So, boundaries and transitions were essential; we need to create buffers that allow us to put one identity aside and then go to another as we move between work and private personas.

Nonetheless, these strange circumstances can bring us closer together, and I think they have allowed us to have other perspectives on the hierarchy and leadership within organizations. Indeed, leaders reported having felt more belonging to their teams since the lockdown. These exceptional circumstances have made it possible to rediscover colleagues, meet others who were strangers to us, and bring us closer.

Working From Home

My purpose in undertaking this research was to capture each participant's current belonging experience. The interviews during the of lockdown seemed to show that people had time to breathe, take stock, and care for themselves.

What was interesting was how many realized how work relationships give us a sense of belonging, continuity, and stability. They anchor us firmly to the ground. The feeling of organizational belonging comes from exchanges between employees. At a time when everyone is isolated and socially distancing, it seems that the need for organizational belonging has heightened. Those participants who did not have a partner or children were particularly susceptible and sensitive to the feeling of not belonging to the team or not seeing them.

Organizations are having to face massive changes, both economically and emotionally. The coronavirus has prompted organizations to significantly expand remote working. There have been hundreds of articles about how to manage the new work environment. Newspapers and magazines talk relentlessly about how you can give meaning to teamwork and value the work of your employees.

Working from home has shown us who the real leaders are in business and who are not. At a time when it is only possible to meet up with each other via videoconferencing, some managers seem to have become more aware both of the extent to which the feeling of belonging to a community is held dear, and also how fragile it is. Teleworking has also revealed to managers that maintaining a strong team spirit must be part of their daily concerns, and that merely working in the same space or organizing one-off events (like annual seminars) cannot be enough.

This period highlights the need to create regular appointments in suitable workspaces (or online) to maintain an attachment to colleagues and enhance the collaborative experience. To do this, visual management tools such as morning stand-up meetings, weekly dashboards posted in the common room or intranet, or the practice of collective feedback will prove to be valuable aids when resuming activity.

Leadership Accountability for Maintaining Belonging Remotely

Even before the pandemic, many organizations had been encouraging their staff to work remotely to reduce real estate costs. This option will likely become even more attractive once the crisis is over. Organizations and managers will have to be deliberate in their responses to this new norm.

Some of the themes noted in my interviews might give some guidance here:

- Employees have a strong need for *group identity*. This is important for work teams, as identification with a group is the foundation for organizational belonging. Belonging can exist even when employees work remotely, and it is needed now more than ever, as it makes them feel protected and secure.
- The need for *emotional resilience and coping strategies* for remote workers should not be underestimated. Respect, active listening, proper airing of differences, laughter, self-awareness, kindness, and compassion will be the tools required by leaders and employees alike.
- A new mindset for everyone in organizations has to be one *of social responsibility.* We are all parts of the whole, and we are all responsible for the whole. We are not separate, working in isolation or in competition with other divisions, business units or even countries. Even if we do not have the *authority*, we all must take responsibility for the well-being of the team and in turn the global health of the organization.

Adaptation is the key to success.
Here are some tips to keep in mind:

1. *Face time.* Try and communicate with your team face to face as much as you can. It allows you to read body language, assess levels of understanding, and build relationships. Leaders must be mood sensors, quickly picking up and identifying subtle signals and changes in work climate and atmosphere. Remember to allow all the voices in your team to be heard—this is especially important for more introverted, quiet team members.
2. *Crystal clear.* Be clear about your intentions. It is only when you are clear about what you want that you can you direct your team. While empathy is important, so too is *hard empathy*: providing employees with what they need to develop their projects and be productive, not just giving them what they want. This authentic approach can help improve performance for you and your team.

3. *A matter of trust.* Hope builds over time and with every action, and trust has to be earned. Make sure you are accountable for your efforts and upfront in your dealings with others. Remember that you do not have to be perfect—sometimes acknowledging your own vulnerabilities can build trust and stimulate a more energetic and collaborative atmosphere.

4. *Walk a mile in their shoes.* As an effective leader, you need to be able to understand your team's perspectives. It is more important than ever to regularly *check in* with your team members, asking and actively listening to find out what is happening with them, personally and workwise. This is surely a time to realize that *the whole person* comes to work, not just a work persona.

It is in the present moment that we build the future, and I think there is a unique opportunity now to question ourselves profoundly and to put people at the center.

Individual Accountability in the New Normal
Controlling Our Responses

The coronavirus pandemic poses a severe challenge to humanity's fundamental structures of collective interconnection. The only thing we can control is how we respond. As Jean-Paul Sartre, French philosopher and novelist, so wisely said, "Life is C between B and D"—"Life is Choice between Birth and Death." This situation is no different—we are faced with choices.

Perhaps, this is the time to look at some of our personal coping strategies and our underpinning thinking about belonging and to consider how these determine the choices that we make and the results that we experience?

We cannot always control the things that happen to us. COVID-19 has certainly taught us that lesson. But we can control the way we think and talk about them. We can exercise control over our interpretations and over the way we perceive the situations that come to us. We can choose to look at things from a different perspective so that we can analyze them more accurately and effectively.

Some simple—although not necessarily easy—techniques include evaluating our biases, reframing, and mindfulness.

Evaluating Cognitive Biases

We have already talked about cognitive biases and how they get in the way of belonging. Taking responsibility for our thinking and identifying where we may be setting up barriers to belonging is not easy, but it is something we can control if we choose to.

It might be difficult to shift our biases, as we do not like to change our thinking patterns. However, in a diverse team, there will be multiple differences and points of view. Establishing a culture of inclusion and belonging requires addressing our biases and really *hearing* what others are saying, especially if we do not agree with them.

Reframing

Someone said: "10 percent of life is made up of what happens to you. 90 percent of life is decided by how you react." If your subconscious mind is filled with negativity, then regardless of what the actual situation is, your response is also likely to be negative. You can change this by reframing the way you see the situation. One definition of reframing is:

Cognitive reframing is a psychological technique that consists of identifying and then changing the way situations, experiences, events, ideas and/or emotions are viewed. Cognitive reframing is the process by which such situations or thoughts are challenged and then changed.

One method to help us reframe is mindfulness practice. Mindfulness is to live in the moment. This means screening out all distractions and giving attention only to what you choose to. For example, if you are jogging, you think only about the jogging itself, its rhythm, the sound of your feet on the ground—and deliberately close out any other thoughts. You can practice mindfulness any time you feel stress and anxiety taking over. Simply stop what you are doing and make yourself mindful by paying attention to what you have selected in your environment. Inhale and take a deep and cleansing breath, and let everything go ... all of the stress, all of the thoughts, and all of the anxiety. As you feel your mind and body relaxing, ease into the stillness and the quiet.

Be Here Now

Some people find mindfulness a challenge, especially at work, so here is some further support on how to remain in the present:

1. Explore what is stressing you: View your situation with positive eyes.
2. Find what you can change: If you could, what parts of your situation would you most like to change? With positive reframing, you may see possibilities you were not aware of before.
3. Identify benefits: Find the benefits in the situation you face.
4. Discover the humor. Find the aspects of your situation that are so absurd that you cannot help but laugh (The Resilience Alliance 2011).

Findings and Quotes From My Research

Remote work

The phenomenon of remote work satisfies the need for autonomy of the new generations. However, developing a sense of belonging is particularly challenging when communication is carried out through e-mails, chat, telephone, or telepresence meetings.

> *I am introverted and have always lived alone and worked remotely. I think we are at the highest risk of feeling a lack of belonging in an organization due to little social interaction and contact with the home office.*
>
> —Food Scientist, FMCG

> *We live in a world where it's important to belong not just physically but digitally too.*
>
> —Head of Diversity and Inclusion, Media Industry

Since the Coronavirus, the belonging part of my family, my nuclear family, is huge. I know we are with ourselves all the time but the connection with the other gives you this internal satisfaction of allowing you to be yourself with yourself. "Self-compassion is a powerful built-in coping system we all have..."

—Psychotherapist

One participant points out how challenging it is to give feedback when employees are miles away, especially when it is performance feedback and must be done via videoconference. Those companies that promote remote work will have to invest in mechanisms to develop a sense of belonging among their employees around the world.

The goal of all leaders or people managers is to bring teams together and make collaboration simple and manageable.

—Headhunter, Recruitment

Remote managers will have to take on the role of community manager. The remote manager is already a manager of tomorrow.

—Director, Airline Industry

Regardless of how well connected you may be, you still must invest time and effort to maintain your relationship. If there is a chance, invite them to visit your company office for a face-to-face meeting. That way, you will establish a trustful relationship by talking about aspirations, fears or hobbies. It will remind them that they're not alone but a part of the team.

—Director of Accounting, News and Media

There is a need to recognize the emotional needs of employees, and especially the emotional stresses that confinement and remote work have created.

I think it's time for a new form of management. What if I pay more attention to our emotions than to our losses? What's at stake? In my view, nothing.

—Journalist, Media

Having poor emotional conditions since confinement is destructive to the core. It is difficult to do our jobs well …. not to mention the internal stress it creates. I feel my sense of wellbeing has declined.

—Finance Professional, Banking

At the end of the day, belonging has benefits for both the individual and the organization, and particularly because individuals who feel they belong become more proactive in dealing with work issues.

Developing a sense of belonging for your team is important whether we are working face to face or remotely. For the individual, 'feeling like you belong', and not just 'knowing you belong' makes all the difference, as it mobilizes more skills, motivation and creativity. For the organization, the benefit is significant because if the feeling of belonging is sufficient, employees will tend to get in touch with each other more efficiently, to take initiatives and to pick up the phone or request a meeting instead of sending an email to solve a problem, show disagreement, or pretend to deal with a subject.

—Head of Digitalization FMCG

Managing Not Belonging in Organizations

Those who feel, or have felt, a lack of belonging in the organization, deal with it in different ways. Some find other employment alternatives as a way to recover their mental and physical health. Others turn to alcohol. Yet others try to change their identities in the effort to belong.

I had to change who I was when I worked in my last organization. It was so fatiguing, and only now I realize how much it impacted my physical health.

—Head of Engineering and Design, Webservices

Another way is to go to a therapist, family, or friends. Sharing experiences with others can help individuals cope with the situation.

Oher participants are more resilient in handling this situation and believe it is necessary to change one's fundamental thinking about work.

One way of thinking about work is that it is an integral part of the lives of individuals. They define their own identity according to the role they play at work or in their profession, and their self-esteem depends on it.

> *Work plays an important role in the life of each individual. To find meaning in one's life, one must find meaning in one's work.*
>
> —Team Lead, Manufacturing Industry

A different view is that this is a mistake, and that individuals can be more self-reliant.

> *Those who rely entirely on work for their self-esteem make a big mistake because if they fail or disappoint, their personal image will be damaged. By conditioning one's self-esteem on professional success, one puts oneself in unnecessary danger.*
>
> —CEO, Banking Industry

This view suggests people can take advantage of rejection to get to know themselves, to identify what they are good at, what they like. The key is to accept themselves; to be kind and compassionate with themselves. Rejection is also seen as a call to action; it can be used to improve work habits and improve relationships with team members.

> *I would encourage you to become conscious, become self-aware and be intentional about what you want. I was unhappy and became angry—then I actually realized I was wasting my energy.*
>
> —Project Manager, Energy Industry

> *For me personally, one of the best ways to handle it is to make sure that I am not adding to the rejection by rejecting myself. It's very easy to take it personally and it's vital for me to always remember to be kind to myself and not internalize the feedback if it's not useful criticism. Rejection helps me clarify where to spend my time and energy. It allows me to focus on opportunities and relationships that prioritize my values and strengths.*
>
> —Physicist, Nuclear Research

CHAPTER 9

The Power of Belonging— The How

If inclusion is being given a seat at the table, belonging is knowing that place is always there for you; whoever you are and however you show up.

—Sunita Sehmi

After reading this far, hopefully many of you might be saying, "OK, I get it." You have a better understanding of what a sense of belonging is all about and why it is important to you as a leader. And now, you are saying, "So what can I do to create a culture of belonging in my organization?" My aim was to give you sufficient information to go from learning to application to integration, and I would like to think of it as a leadership journey not a destination. In this chapter, I will give some additional recommendations based on my own experience and from my research on how to develop belonging in teams and organizations.

Great teams and individuals need an exceptional measure of emotional intelligence; from there, they make up the collective intelligence. Numerous studies show that emotional intelligence is essential to group success.

Building Relationships

Some of the elements of emotional intelligence I think are important to building relationships are:

- Interpersonal skills: Knowing how to get along with others.
- Intrapersonal skills: Understanding yourself, self-awareness.
- Flexibility: The ability to adapt to the realities around you and to make the changes that are required if you are to be more effective.

- Stress tolerance: Things are just not going to go your way all of the time, and you need to be able to deal with this.
- Mood management: Knowing that you choose your mood, regardless of the circumstances.

Connection

In April 2010, Hedy Schleifer gave a TEDx Talk in Tel Aviv. Her message is both inspiring and powerful. She communicates the notion that there are three invisible connectors: the space, the bridge, and the encounter. When people make these three hidden connectors visible in their lives and embrace them fully, the *miracle* of connection happens. The space is the relational space between people. To respect that space, one must cross the bridge and bring one's full and authentic presence to the world of the *other*. In doing so, the perfect conditions are established to create a genuine encounter of the souls. Once the space has been honored and the bridge has been crossed, an honest, wholesome, and fulfilling bond is established. You are present; you listen to the other, with the only aim being to understand the other.

Hedy cites philosopher Martin Buber: "It is our relationships that live in the space between us." This space is crucial to creating real relations. Hedy says that we frequently unconsciously contaminate "the space between us" by inserting a cutting look, a criticism, or a complaint. We must continually be mindful of what we put into the space, choosing to put positivity and a smile into the space.

In our global world, whoever and wherever we are, we need to all cross *the bridge*, remembering that you cannot bring anything of yours to the other side. You bring just yourself and listen and watch with new eyes and new ears.

Similarities

In my experience, a highly effective technique is to focus on similarities, what you have in common, instead of concentrating on difference. By driving connection based on similarities, you can create an interpersonal environment that is psychologically safer for the other and yourself.

In this environment, *making a mistake* is not held against you, and you are more likely to use it as an opportunity to better understand each other. It takes courage and willingness to get past barriers, but you will be surprised at how effective it can be to look past apparent differences and focus instead on the things you share.

How we connect on these parallels is central to all human relationships. This subtle twist in perspective can have some pretty powerful effects. The more people I meet and work with, the more I recognize how many experiences and emotions we share. Despite our cultural, gender, cognitive and geographical differences, there are many commonalities that we can all embrace. Yet, life is so demanding that we often do not have time to be mindful of the universal realities that touch all our lives, whoever and wherever we are. What makes us forget these common denominators is often a feeling that we are the only ones going through tough times.

Whatever our *reality*, there are certain truths that are common to humankind; they are shared and valid at all times wherever you are in the world:

1. We all want to avoid suffering for ourselves and for the ones we love. We will all do our best to prevent suffering and have an enriched life.
2. We all worry about our children and want the best for them. We all want them to make the right choices; we all want to protect them and keep them from harm.
3. We are all affected by stress at some point in our life. It is an inevitable part of life and reality. Of course, stress can represent different things to different people, but no one escapes. It touches all of our lives. How we deal with it is a personal matter, but this is a struggle we all face, wherever we are.
4. We all need love and recognition. No matter who we are or where we are, love is a feeling that we all want to experience. Feeling loved validates us and helps us to feel important. Whenever we do not understand others or feel detached from them, we need to remind ourselves that they too, just like us, want to be loved and accepted. I have never met anyone who disagrees with this life truth.
5. We struggle to accept that we cannot control our lives 100 percent of the time. Change is difficult to adapt to, adjust to, and accommodate.

In this ever-changing world, coping with change is an ever-present battle.

6. We all want to belong and feel part of the group, to be included and involved. This is a fundamental need.

Moving the Needle

The starting point for establishing a changed approach to belonging in the workplace is understanding and accepting where you are right now—where is the needle of inclusion on the organization's dashboard?

The next step is understanding and accepting that all organizations can have as many initiatives and policies as they want, but moving the needle starts with you. It is never somebody else's problem. Care and understanding are very important for every individual—experiencing it and showing it to others.

What makes this hard is the fact that it is still difficult to discuss emotions at work. Once we acknowledge this difficulty, we need to dig deep to root it out.

One fundamental practice is to talk about the elephant in the room. Having the courage to call it out is critical. At the same time, psychological safety is always paramount; therefore, the *way* we *call things out* or challenge is just as critical. When leaders get this wrong, team members are quick to spot lack of authenticity and poor alignment of actions and values.

Issues around inclusion and exclusion, belonging or not-belonging are often avoided or ignored, even when it is obvious that they are causing difficulties in a group or team.

Our natural reaction is to avoid discomfort and difficult conversations, and sadly, this only creates more problems down the line. It is interesting what stories we tell ourselves to avoid taking responsibility. This is why, belonging initiatives should not be approached as standalone. Rather, they should form part of and be integrated into all team activities. An endorsement of this approach from senior leaders or managers and the *tone from the top* is critical and sends a clear message.

The emphasis must be on articulating the clear business benefits of a coherent strategy across the organization, as this is the best way to achieve full buy-in. Everyone knows that a sense of belonging is a *good* thing, but it is necessary to have the organization truly embrace it, live it, and prioritize it. The power at the top has to believe it will be of tangible benefit for themselves and for the organization as a whole. And, that means clearly stating what belonging means for the organization and providing clear support for the diversity and inclusion (D&I) office, if there is one.

The challenge to leaders—and in fact to everyone in the organization—is to be aware of current social issues and to review the content of case studies and resources currently being used in the organization.

Nothing is in isolation, and so, creating a true culture of belonging cannot be decreed or imposed. It must be prepared, cocreated, and cultivated. And yes, there is a high possibility that several critical conversations will have to take place. Because before a breakthrough, there has to be a breakdown. This means that an organization and its leaders should determine the tools and the structure for collective reflection that, hopefully, will lead to action for the benefit of each individual and the group. All in all, the pivotal goal is to promote visibility and recognition of each person's contribution.

At an Individual Level

1. **Not enough time**.

   Yes, these conversations take time. It takes time to set a leadership ethos, what you will bear and for how long. But, the payback is impactful and useful and, in the long term, you will save time.

2. **I might make it worse by saying something.**

   Saying nothing at all is worse. Silence gives consent to bad behavior. You have to start somewhere and better out than in. You create the team tone, what is safe to talk about and what is not.

3. **The project will not struggle if I do not say anything.**

   Oh yes, it will. People will work, but not at the same level of enthusiasm, energy, and vigor.

4. **I am not skilled enough on this topic.**

   Not being an expert does not mean you do not know the right thing to do. The whole topic of D&I is about people, care, and compassion. If you are not skilled in that, you should not be a leader.

5. **It is not my responsibility.**

Oh yes, it is. We are all responsible, especially you! You are account-able and answerable to your team. You are responsible for:

- Keeping it real
- Keeping it relevant
- Keeping it safe

At a Team Level

Here are reminders for leaders:

1. Have positive intent for one another. Assuming positive intent means continuously beginning from the knowledge that your col-league means well and is doing their best, no matter what they say or do.
2. Communication is better than no communication. So, do not be afraid to talk; it is essential for building strong relationships. With-out authentic communication, relationships can turn bitter and lead to skepticism and errors.
3. Accept and talk about differences within the team; together, with focus on one common objective, it is possible to form an integrated, reliable, and credible *team* versus a *group* of individuals separated by divides.
4. Create a group mentoring or feedback culture, which enables people to lead from their strengths, to grow and develop themselves and others.

At an Organizational Level

1. *Make belonging a strategic imperative of the organization*: Treat belong-ing as a compelling business case, making it a strategic imperative of the organization.
2. *Walk the Talk Leadership*: Implement how to manage belonging coaching for all people leaders.
3. *Engrain the importance of belonging in the employment procedures*: Ana-lyze the current hiring practices of your organization; this includes

sourcing, recruiting, and interviewing. Are they truly reflecting an authentic and belonging culture?

4. *Embed belonging in talent management*: Make sure that displaying belonging behaviors is mirrored in both performance-based evaluations, promotions, and succession planning. Make sure your talent has a deep understanding and commitment on creating a belonging culture.

5. *Provide support, guidance on belonging*: Identify where the gaps are in the organization and offer to measure the satisfaction level of target groups who participate in the training. This should start from the top! CEO and executive committee must walk the talk and lead by example. Such leaders show greater congruence between intent and action. Successful programs for executives should go from learning to integration. Working on a deep dive, acknowledging thoughts, emotions, and habits, and understanding our blind spots.

6. *Establish a corporate culture and employee conduct into the topic of belonging—internally and externally*: When an organization has implemented the levers as their guiding values, it becomes easier to change their practices to having a belonging culture. When integrating a new employee, it is vital to convey the central values of the company. In addition to the introduction to colleagues with whom the recruit will be working, providing them with a 'survival' pack will ensure a smooth transition. A new colleague who develops a sense of belonging can promote the corporate culture. To attract potential candidates, the culture of belonging within the company must be highlighted in the recruitment campaign.

The feeling of belonging to an organization is the identification and specific attachment to a reference group rendering to universal values and characteristics. Indeed, the more the sense of belonging is present, the more the employees are motivated and driven.

Membership of reference groups represents a group of individuals who share common characteristics such as age, gender, education, or social background. All the members of a social group must be aware of belonging to this group and must interact more or less directly with each other and therefore, distinguish a social group from a simple grouping of some individuals.

Reflective Exercise

This a question I regularly ask in workshops: Think back to a time when you should have addressed a belonging issue at work and did not.

- *Why didn't you?*
- *What was the difficulty?*
- *What could have made it easier for you to do so?*

Findings and Quotes From My Research

Strategies to Develop a Sense of Belonging in Organizations

Participants agree that managers and leaders play a determining role in developing a sense of belonging in the organization. The responsibility for creating a collective consciousness around the values, mission, and goals of the organization falls on them; it is up to them to create an inclusive environment where employees feel safe to share their ideas; to promote spaces to develop connections between team members, where they recognize their differences and accept each other; and to motivate teams to do their best. It is clear to the participants that the relationship with the manager or leader can impact productivity and employee commitment to the organization.

Based on their current or past experiences, participants described some actions that managers or leaders can take to develop a sense of belonging in the organization.

Listen to Employees

Managers or leaders should listen to the concerns of employees and show interest in knowing their values, experiences, perspectives, and the environment outside of the workplace. They can ask about their families, what changes they would like in the tasks they perform, what their qualities and strengths are. To do this requires confidence from managers and leaders.

> *I can't believe my boss brought our team together to talk about a project he wants to implement. He wanted to ask our opinion on it...Ours! We're just handlers.' When an employee says this to me, I understand*

that this boss invests in his employees' sense of belonging and that they will want to continue to do a good job and much more.
                              —Executive Committee Member, Finance Industry

Recognize the Work of Employees

Recognizing the value of employees' work—individual and collective—is a vital motivator to improved performance and retention of talent.

The manager or leader can congratulate and thank them. One participant proposed selecting an *employee of the month*.

> *As far as employers are concerned, a message of encouragement, congratulations or thanks is always pleasing and motivating.*
> —Head of Security, Tech

The form of recognition may vary according to the personality of each employee.

> *At work, recognition gives us a sense of belonging to a group and allows us to build social self-esteem. But we are not all equal in the face of this desire: to be persuaded of the value of their productions, some need to be told ten times in a row. Others want to be recognized in public, not face-to-face: the trumpets of fame need to resound.*
> —Deputy Head, Science

Celebrating the success of a project is also a form of recognition. It is a strategy that strengthens the bonds between team members and reinforces the collective consciousness.

Writing down the project results on a whiteboard is one way to accomplish this.

> *Celebrating successes, such as hitting targets, reaching goals, and landing new clients, fosters strong bonds within a team or department. It gives the employees the chance to reflect on their teamwork and appreciate what they have achieved together. We take the time to bring people together to enjoy their collective success.*
> —Yoga instructor, Wellbeing

When we "win" a project, the CEO comes in and rings a big cowbell to announce the good news. It's a strategy that allows employees to rejoice collectively and creates a sense of belonging.

—Philosophy Lecturer, University

Create Spaces to Interact

When managers and leaders are honest and transparent in their emotions, this gives employees the confidence to communicate their own concerns and ideas. For this to happen requires that there are spaces where they can interact. Christmas parties, birthday celebrations, lunchtimes, and special activities outside the office—such as sports activities—are some spaces proposed by the participants where employees are given *the opportunity to exist in the group*. It is in these spaces that inclusion and acceptance and the strengthening of ties between team members can be promoted. There they can share the same reality.

Sharing some personal time with people around a meal is a perfect way to build connections, which then serves to smooth the business path.

—CEO, Communications

Several of the companies I worked for made efforts in this direction: Christmas parties or other parties; activities outside the office (corporate retreats); celebrating birthdays; gifts of all kinds.

—Economist, Finance Industry

Define Goals and Responsibilities

Participants believed that employees need to know that they are part of the puzzle. So, it is important to share the organization's vision and objectives with them. The manager or leader must give clarity in the assigned tasks and responsibilities and define the roles. Certainty about the work they are doing allows employees to have a clear image of what their contribution will be. This gives them a common purpose and reinforces collective identity; it is a motivator.

I see a lack of vision on the part of managers who do not consider it necessary to have a clear, strong and inspiring mission for the team.
                                    —Project Coordinator, Insurance

Train Leaders

To ensure that managers or leaders can develop a sense of belonging among team members, the organization must ensure that they acquire the knowledge, skills, and tools necessary to create an inclusive environment, to strengthen ties between team members, and to guide employees toward the same purpose. The manager or leader must understand what a sense of belonging means to talk about it with employees and lead by example.

Building trust is essential and engaging in dialogue about belonging and inclusion can be very personal. So, engaging in such discussions with some background knowledge will help you build trust and communicate effectively. You will demonstrate that you are serious about creating an inclusive workplace culture.
                        —Human Rights Officer, International Organization

CHAPTER 10

Longing for Belonging

Inclusion is about the here and now, belonging continues even when the team is not together.

—Sunita Sehmi

Belonging is vital for our emotional and physical health and plays a big part in the way we reason and cooperate with the world. The way we engage with others is fundamental to our civilization. Belonging is an asset in your organization and in your team, so wear it as a badge of integrity, because when you make your people feel that they can say what they need to say, be who they need to be, act as they need to act and still feel welcomed and included for being their unique authentic selves, that is your organizational wealth, and it is something to be preserved, maintained, and treasured.

Organizations recognize that not belonging is always an issue, but sometimes, they fail to make headway. Although the organizations are committed and endeavoring to get the message out, the response and the reality are less favorable.

Diversity, inclusion, and belonging are acknowledged sources of creativity and innovation that can improve performance and ultimately create a definite advantage for an organization. However, organizations still need to capitalize on a greater diverse workforce and create the right environment where differences become an asset that leads to creativity, idea generation and, ultimately, innovation.

When you're having a tough day or struggling with something, imagine a friend or family member coming to you and asking how you are. That's belonging.

—Legal Director, Multinational

Be the Change You Wish to See

People want to see themselves represented in their organizations. When there is a lack of diversity and we do not see people like ourselves across the organization, there is a missing piece to diversity and inclusion. It is not enough to be included. We all need to belong.

We know that a sense of belonging in organizations is related to the human need to establish connections with other people. It has a strong affective component: individuals seek affection, love, protection, and support and find it in social groups with which they share the same interests and beliefs. However, as the workplace is a space where individuals with diverse ideas and cultures interact, the organization must be an environment where all employees can establish connections and feel the confidence to express themselves freely. In other words, they must not just be included—they must belong. This is especially true now with the coronavirus pandemic, where people have fears about losses and changes and what that means for employees.

When employees can identify with the benefits of their organization and identify with its mission and goals, this intensifies their sense of belonging. Thus, it is essential for organizations to create a collective awareness around a common purpose and to recognize the contribution of each member of the team. I often feel that work and indeed the world would be a better place if we *replaced hostility with curiosity.*

Teamwork is important, and organizations thrive when teams are trusted to create, debate, and collaborate. Indeed, Deloitte's research into organizational performance has shown that shifting toward a team-based organizational model improves performance, often significantly. Throughout my research, I observed that being part of a group and being accepted by others is a basic need; even more, being part of a community is vital to our well-being. What was interesting was the general theme of being alone, feeling invisible, and emotional pain.

Longing for Belonging?

This approach is based on trust and the trustworthiness of those who nurture it. It requires an example of committing to creating a culture of belonging in the top echelons in organizations, sponsoring of a culture of belonging, and holding the levers of the organization responsible. Moreover, by integrating these points, you can help others become accountable and responsible for themselves and then others too. And so, the current begins to cascade transversely across and throughout the organization.

Many attempts to implement diversity programs have *failed spectacularly*, according to an article in the *Harvard Business Review*. There could be many reasons for this, but, in my view, what is missing from many diversity and inclusion roadmaps is the fact that people need to belong. People need to feel that they matter. People need to think that they can be who they are. I have myself experienced both a true sense of belonging in teams and organizations and a sense of nonbelonging, and I have triumphed and suffered, respectively.

Belonging is a feeling that lasts even when we are not physically present, and I think what is essential is to be mindful, responsible, and accountable. We saw from my research how belonging impacts motivation and engagement. So, your people turn up to work—but do you have their full engagement?

The Power of Belonging

My data illustrates that adopting team structures improves organizational performance. Whether teams are based in Mumbai or Munich, Copenhagen or Cape Town, teams get things done when they work well as a collective. Teams are the core energy that drive our organizations.

Specific personal characteristics are shown to promote the development of a sense of belonging, namely: the desire to achieve professional fulfillment, a sense of responsibility, and self-esteem. So, despite an employer's best efforts, there will be some employees who are incapable of developing a strong sense of belonging to the organization.

Increasingly, I believe self-acceptance is the foundation of a sense of belonging. *True belonging starts with us, knowing who we are and what we stand for.* The most difficult lesson to learn perhaps is that belonging will remain a puzzle until we find that it has a personal dwelling place—that we must first belong deeply to ourselves.

Along with this comes personal responsibility for belonging, and clearly, individuals also have some responsibility here. For many, personal baggage gets in the way of assimilating into an organization—the stories they tell themselves are really about the past, and this focus hijacks the reality of the present.

As one of the participants in my research pointed out, organizations cannot create a sense of belonging without the cooperation of employees. And, some participants believed that taking ownership required being courageous and speaking openly about feeling excluded. However, the stigma of being labeled as weak led to ignoring, lack of acknowledging, and indifference.

I believe that when we have a sense that we do not belong, taking ownership may also include being mindful of the possibility that our perceptions of being included or excluded have their roots in our own thinking.

It seems that it is enough to develop a sense of belonging, and motivation and commitment are almost guaranteed to follow. Nonetheless, the feeling of belonging is not permanent; it can fluctuate according to situations that only the organization can influence. Thus, maintaining it is an ongoing effort on the part of the authority figures in the organization.

Leadership Is Heart Work

Our world appears to be becoming more divided between people, countries, genders, cultures, political beliefs, religions, and philosophies broadening at a worrying degree. And, this disengagement is paradoxically generating activities getting people closer together than ever. It takes great strength and courage to remain open-hearted and vulnerable in the world we live in today. Leaders who operate with deliberate compassion and calm are the winners during a crisis. This is not about vulnerability—it is about nondefensiveness. It allows us to be with our feelings. We can be with ourselves and then be with others. Our organizations and our teams provide a supportive environment and caring behavior that create a sense of trust and safety. So, we know that what makes collaboration work is keeping an open mind, listening, being honest and trustworthy. Conversely, what destroys safety, inclusion, and belonging is dishonesty, closed-mindedness, attacking, defending, hiding, and being selfish. Study after study shows that becoming a conscious, attentive leader means paying attention, adopting appropriate leadership styles for different situations, taking responsibility for inclusion.

Primarily, because they know how to manage their fears and remain in control. Indeed, emotions are at the heart of our teams, and yet, they remain the tremendous taboo in organizations. Even though we have seen that managing emotions is a genuine leadership skill, it is not always so natural for some. Let us face it; at a time when the world is in uncertainty, we need all the help we can get.

So how can we limit thinking traps and practice heartfelt leadership? Why are inclusive leaders good for organizations and how do you become one?[1]

Here are some tips to help you.

1. *Be prepared*
   Plans are hopeless, but planning is vital. It serves to improve and secure the right sort of authority.
2. *It is okay to know that you do not know*
   When leaders do that, they are able to harness this interpersonal presence and connect with others' vulnerable side.
3. *In a crisis, be decisive*
   We all need to challenge the rules as a part of our development. Your job is to help your team to strive for success. Challenging individuals is not harmful; instead, it is your responsibility to present existing challenges as opportunities and to be available for support if needed.

---

1 Why Inclusive Leaders Are Good for Organizations, and How to Become One *By Juliet Bourke And Andrea Espedido March 29, 2019.*

4. *Eat lots of humble pie*

According to Professor Edgar Schein[2] of MIT, traditional leadership structures based on static hierarchy, junior workers hold back too often, reluctant to say something that might make them look bad. That is why, hero leadership needs to give way to what Schein calls *humble* leadership, which encourages multiple perspectives.

5. *Empathy*

Empathy is becoming popular in the corporate world, and it is an aspect that covers a much broader and more complex field than kindness. Embedded in a logic of otherness, it qualifies a relationship between two people. A crucial point when it comes to communication. Empathy establishes a link between an I and you. In any human organization, empathetic leadership is valued, appreciated, and welcomed.

6. *Connect*

Initiate bonding and choose to connect with your team. Develop a sincere interest in your team members. This will serve all of you well in the long run, as once people feel connected, your working relationship is likely to improve.

7. *Listen with your whole*

Various studies list listening ability as one of the characteristics of effective leadership. It is one of the main expectations of our employees. Frank Ostaseski[3], a Buddhist teacher, goes a step further. He encourages us to learn to listen and communicate from three levels, the body, the heart, and the mind.

8. *Curiosity did not kill the cat*

You can never overcommunicate in a time of crisis. Keep talking, keep connecting, and keep up the dialogue. But, keep your communication crystal clear. Curiosity is about learning, exploration, and investigation, and there is so much to be gained by being curious in a global setting. Ask questions, discover more, have a thirst for

---

[2] Edgar H. Schein is a professor emeritus from the MIT Sloan School of Management and pioneer in organizational development, organizational culture, and process consulting.

[3] Frank Ostaseski, Buddhist teacher, cofounder of the Zen Hospice Project and founder of the Metta Institute. Author of The Five Invitations

knowledge and your environment. Always ask open-ended *how* and *why* questions and wait for their answers.

9. *Conflict*

Disagreements are part of life, and how we deal with them is often shown by the team leader. Have thin skin, be aware of any disputes and support team members to debate and face conflicts.

10. *Cooperation*

We are all looking for the achievement and practice of working collectively toward a common goal. By doing the aforementioned, you will ensure effective teamwork, a healthy debate, more in-depth inquiry, and a common bond.

11. *Walk the talk*

To care means to feel genuine concern and interest in your team and to ensure you look after and provide for their needs. Simply, this means a real understanding of the difficulty of others and a desire to relieve it. We all need to care about our colleagues, but we need to start with ourselves, that is, we have to be compassionate and mindful of our needs, and the sorrow of saying goodbye to our old life is a must for any leader. So, this means that if you are going to talk the talk, you have got to walk the walk. Because no matter what background, ethnicity, or gender, all of us want to belong. My trajectory of feeling like an outsider, unquestionably set me on a life track to bring all the outsiders into the *ingroup* and give them a sense of belonging. And, what I know for sure is the feeling of not belonging, or not truly recognized, is something we all feel at times to varying degrees, although something that we feel uneasy admitting to. As a consequence of my own life experiences, I have a deep sense that people, including myself, feel unsafe when they do not belong. Because the power of belonging helps us survive and thrive.

What Is the Secret to a True Belonging Culture?

A place where everyone is responsible, and everyone is accountable. We are craving for meaning and authenticity, and people can feel what is authentic and what is not. Think of your team as fellow travelers, rather than lonely passengers. We are all in this together, and small changes make a big difference.

Each one of us regardless of our function at work can become an intentional learner willing to learn and willing to be curious. Despite noble intentions and the knowledge, many leaders strive with how to actualize a belonging workforce because not belonging can manifest itself in many ways, such as nonengagement, bitterness, and sometimes anger.

This then becomes difficult to manage because it requires us to go beyond what we see and ask deeper questions. And, I am inviting you to ask those questions and manage your expectations, as this is a process that takes time, compassion, and heartfelt leadership.

Desmond Tutu put it perfectly, remember "Ubuntu[4]," a term meaning humanity and "I am because we are" is the core of humanity compassion for each another, both in small and large groups.

And, I appreciate that this is a personal journey, and we are all at varying places, but I know for sure we can all do more to make our teams and workplaces and leaders who manage teams have huge impact. When we align our words and actions, we become the conscious creators of our lives and changes.

Creating a conscious culture shift is creating a more connected organization, and this journey begins with a series of important steps, the first is to imagine the organization you wish to operate it, visualize it, cocreate a cognizant roadmap, and be the change you want to see in the world.

So, let me ask you, how are you going to change your world today?

---

[4] Ubuntu (Zulu pronunciation: [ùɓúntʼù]) is a Nguni Bantu term meaning *humanity*. It is often translated as "I am because we are" or "humanity toward others" or in Xhosa, "umntu ngumntu ngabantu," but is often used in a more philosophical sense to mean "the belief in a universal bond of sharing that connects all humanity."

Desmond Tutu Peace Foundation

At a seminar at the University of Leicester regarding "Public Faith in a Secular Age," Archbishop Desmond Tutu describes some of the tenants of the philosophy of Ubuntu. The idea of our interconnectedness with each other. https://youtube.com/watch?v=GaiKX5VdfVE

Afterword

If you would like more information on how to introduce or improve more belonging in your organization, drop me a line at sunita.sehmi@walkthetalk.ch.

Be well always,
Sunita Sehmi

Appendix

Research Project:
The Power of Belonging

This appendix provides some details of the research project that I undertook to explore belonging in organizations and to interrogate and validate the content of my book. It outlines the aims and methodology of the research project, describes the themes that emerged from the responses, and gives some supplementary information, including the preamble to the interviews, the questions asked, and a visualization of the findings.

The Research Setting

Purpose of the Research

The primary purpose of this research project was to explore, investigate, and understand the sense of belonging for individuals in organizations.

The observations from informal focus groups conducted during Diversity and Inclusion workshops contributed to my choice of questions in the interviews. I wanted to hear the stories that people wanted to tell us. And, I wanted to understand how these experiences, in turn, impacted organizational culture and collective behavior and whether we could transform the findings into practical organizational policies and processes.

Preparation Stage

I conducted face-to-face, remote, and telephone interviews consisting of six open-ended questions, including some subquestions, designed to gather as much rich data as possible. The initial questions were devised to gather information about the participant's background while simultaneously trying to form a comfortable relationship. The rest of the questions were intended to explore how important belonging is in an organizational setting.

Participants

I interviewed 129 people, comprising 71 men and 58 women. Participants included professionals from more than 50 countries around the world and from sectors including, among others, health, business, nonprofits, media, and education. They represented a wide range of functions—from a priest to a CEO.

I interviewed 105 participants before the COVID-19 crisis and then another 24 at the beginning of the pandemic. All were promised that their names and companies would not be disclosed.

Preamble to Interviews

Thank you for taking the time to participate in my research. Today's interview is part of a qualitative research project within the framework of my research for my second book.

In particular, this research aims to understand the impact of belonging in your professional activity, namely, at the team and organization level. I am here to hear your views and your personal opinion about the topic of belonging.

Of course, everything that is said during this interview will remain absolutely confidential. If I record it, it is to facilitate our discussion and avoid mistakes in my notetaking.

The duration of the interview should in principle not exceed one hour. I would like to say that there is no right or wrong answer. Before we begin, do you have any questions?

Interview Questions

1. What are your views on belonging in organizations?
2. Is belonging important to your current organization?
3. What is difficult about not belonging in organizations?

4. When has a lack of belonging impacted your well-being? How do or did you manage this?
5. How much support do you have from your management to develop belonging at your work?
6. How important has the role of belonging been in your life?

Data Collection

The interviews were conducted from October 2019 to April 2020. They were semistructured, with everyone being asked the same six questions. The duration of each interview averaged about 30 to 45 minutes. All were recorded and subsequently transcribed. I carefully considered what transpired in each interview to gain a sense of what the research participants were actually revealing about their working lives. I studied not only what they said, but also how they explained their statements and actions, and what I saw and sensed during the interviews.

Themes in the Responses

The findings highlighted what participants understood about the notion of sense of belonging and the ambiguity around how to handle it, particularly in organizational contexts. Themes arose as participants voiced the view that, regardless of their titles, they all had fundamental human needs and emotions, one of which was belonging. Only one participant out of 129 said organizational belonging did not matter to him.

These were the themes and subthemes that emerged:

1. Defining belonging
   • Social relationships based on inclusion, acceptance, and recognition
2. Belonging in organizations
   • Alignment between the values of the organization and employees
3. The positive effects of the sense of belonging in organizations
   • Happiness
   • Well-being

- Engagement
- Motivation
- Loyalty
- Productivity
- Retention

4. The impact of the sense of not belonging
   - Unhappiness
   - Mental and physical health illnesses
   - Loss of motivation and productivity
   - Absenteeism and loss of talents

5. Managing not belonging in organizations

6. Challenges for organizations
   - Diversity
   - Generations Y-Z
   - Remote work
   - Management focused on the individual

7. Strategies to develop a sense of belonging in organizations
   - Listen to employees
   - Recognize the work of employees
   - Create spaces to interact
   - Define goals and responsibilities
   - Train leaders

Visualization of Findings

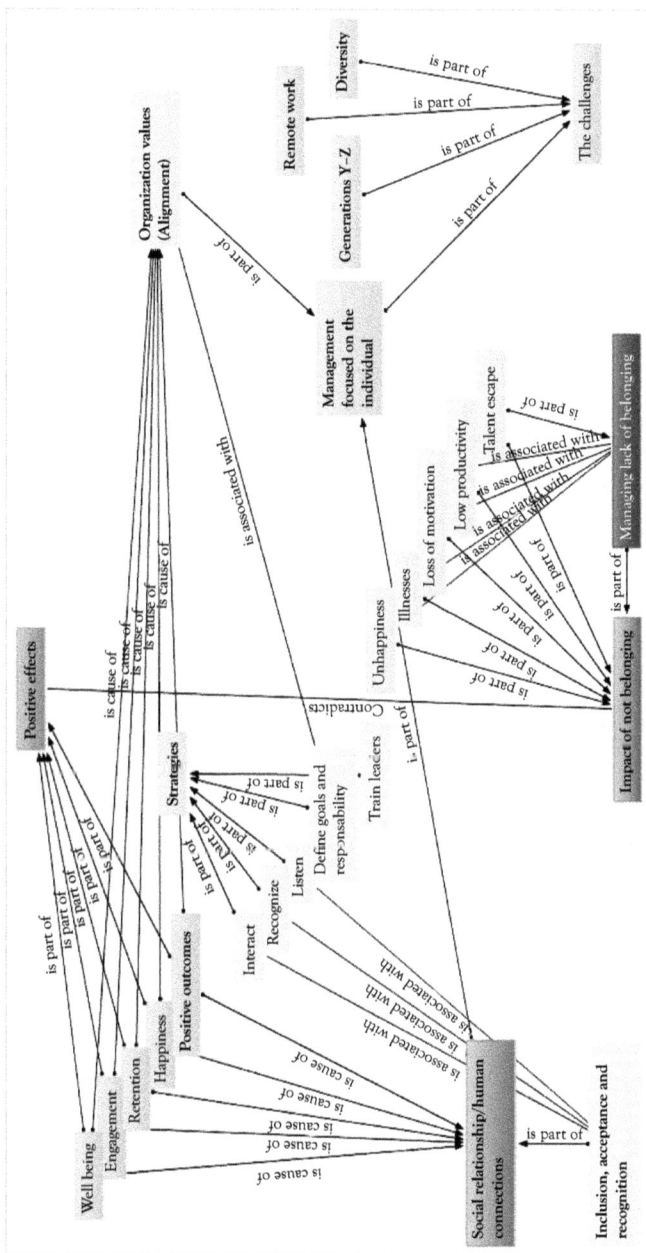

Figure A.1 Positive outcomes

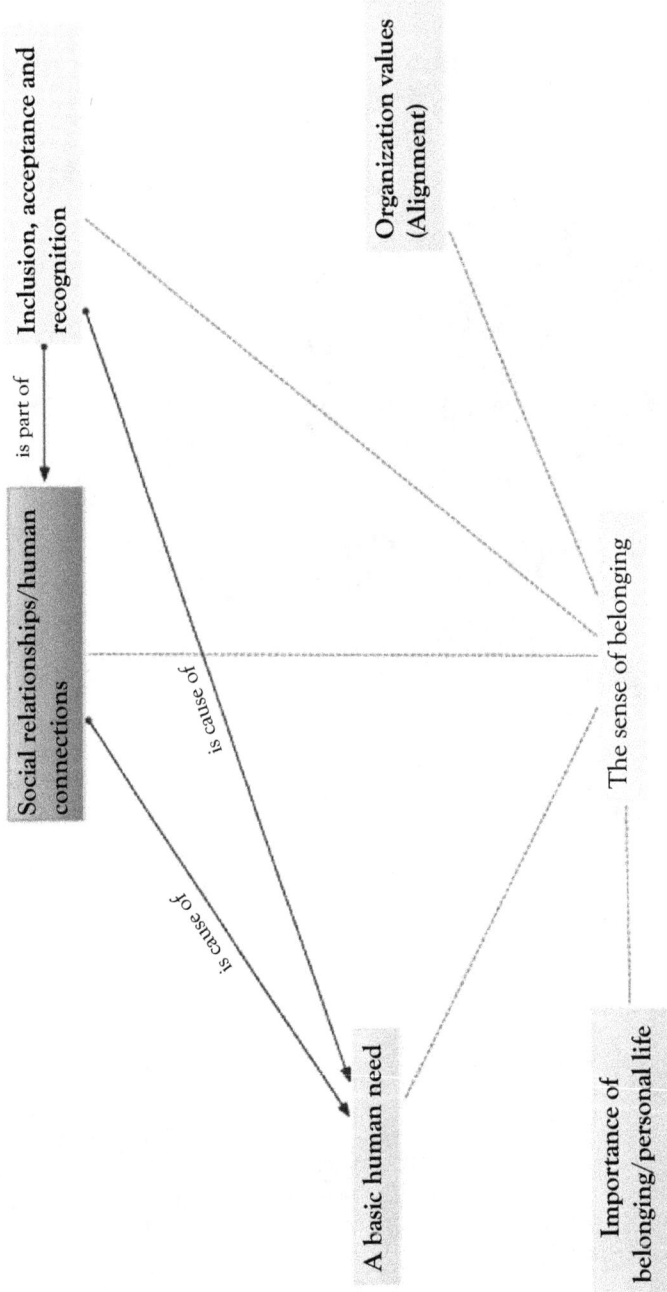

Figure A.2 Belonging, social relationships, and alignment with the values of the organization

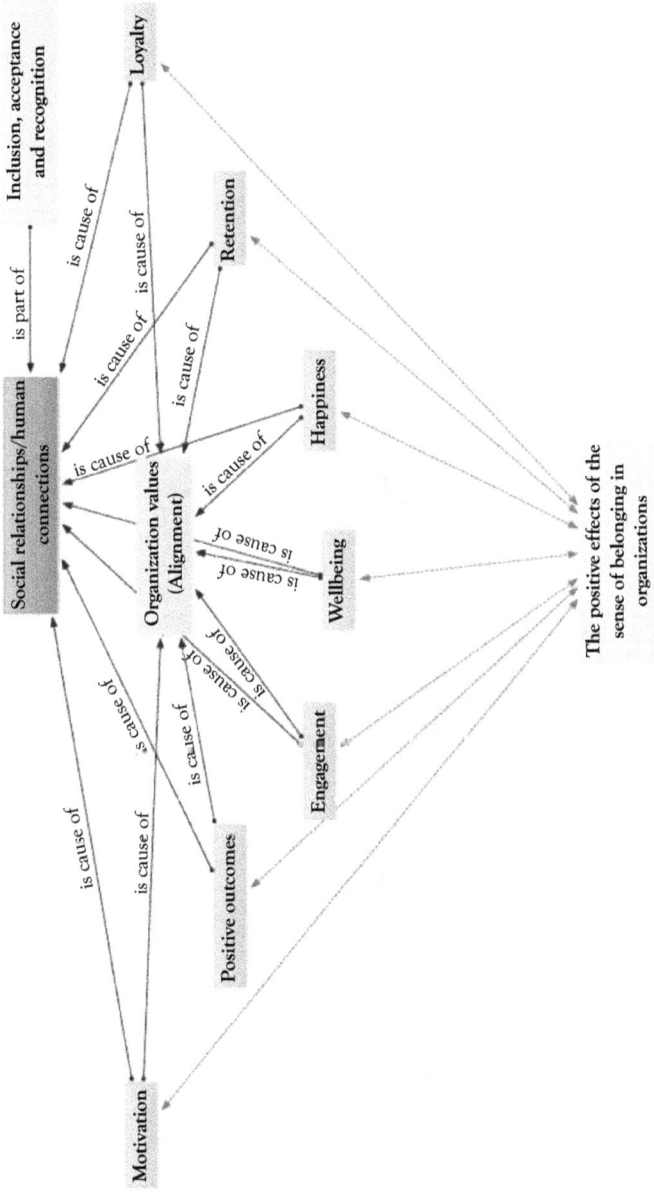

Figure A.3 The positive effects of belonging in organizations

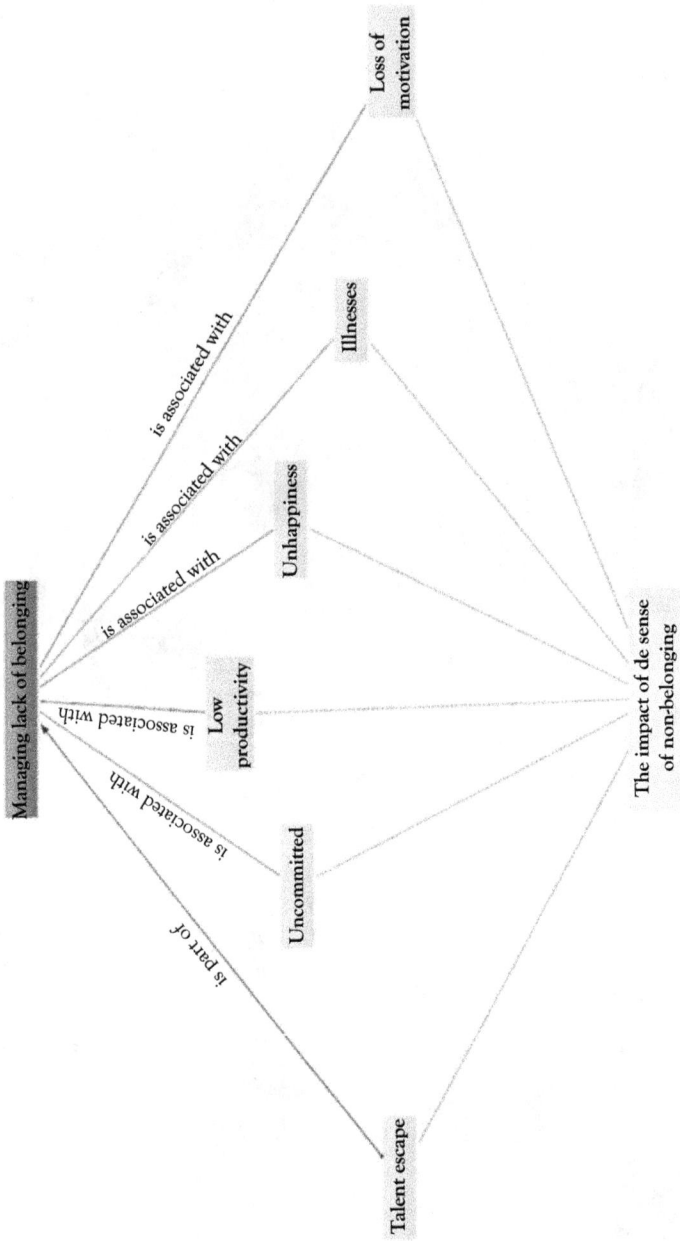

Figure A.4 The impact of nonbelonging

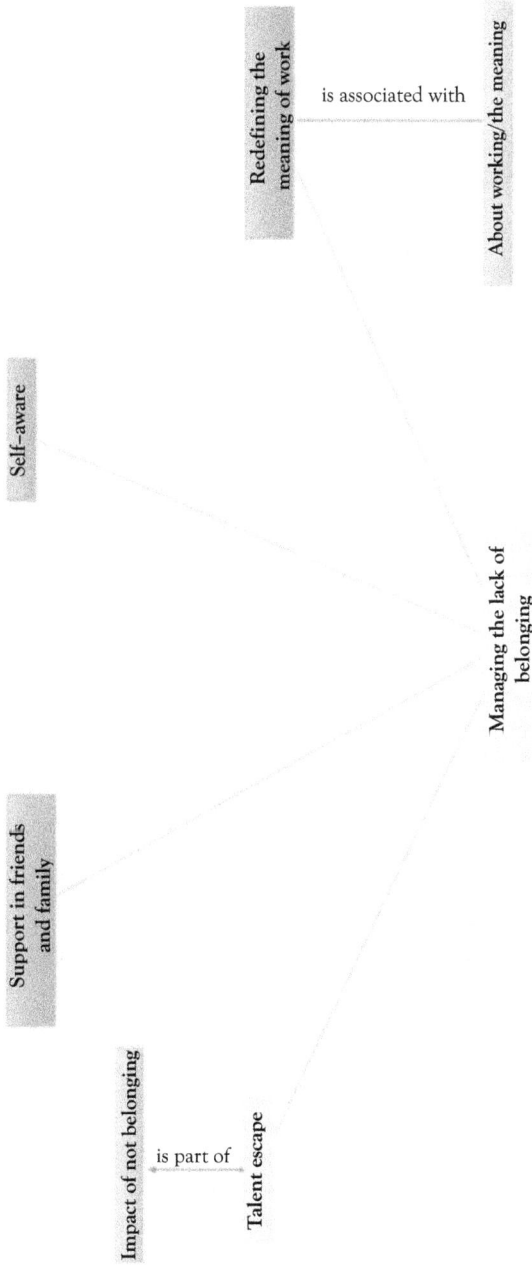

Figure A.5 Managing nonbelonging in organizations

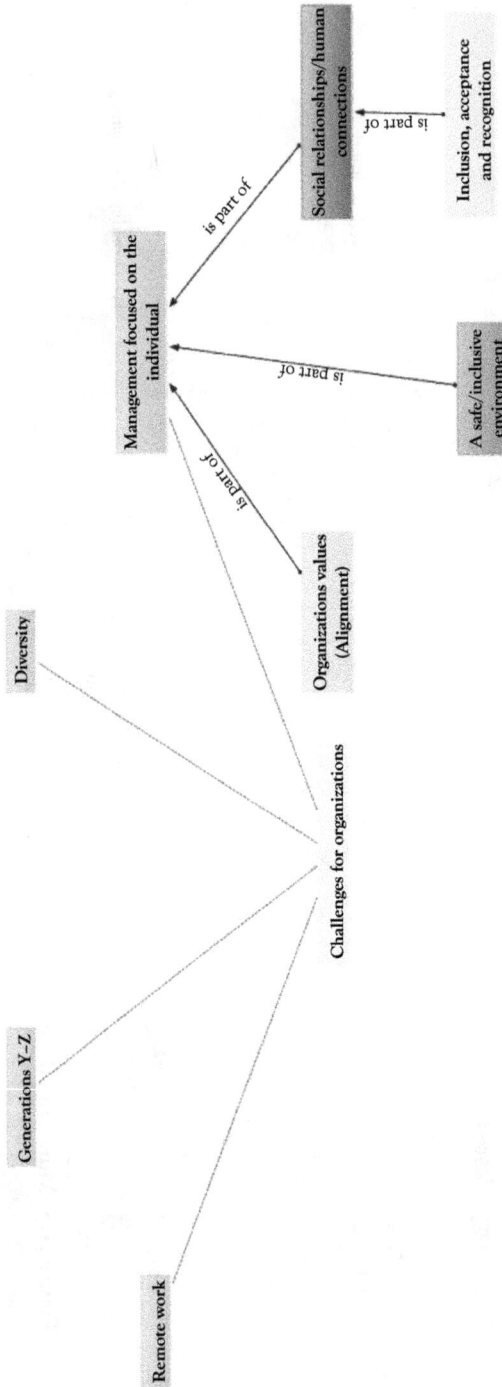

Figure A.6 Challenges for organizations

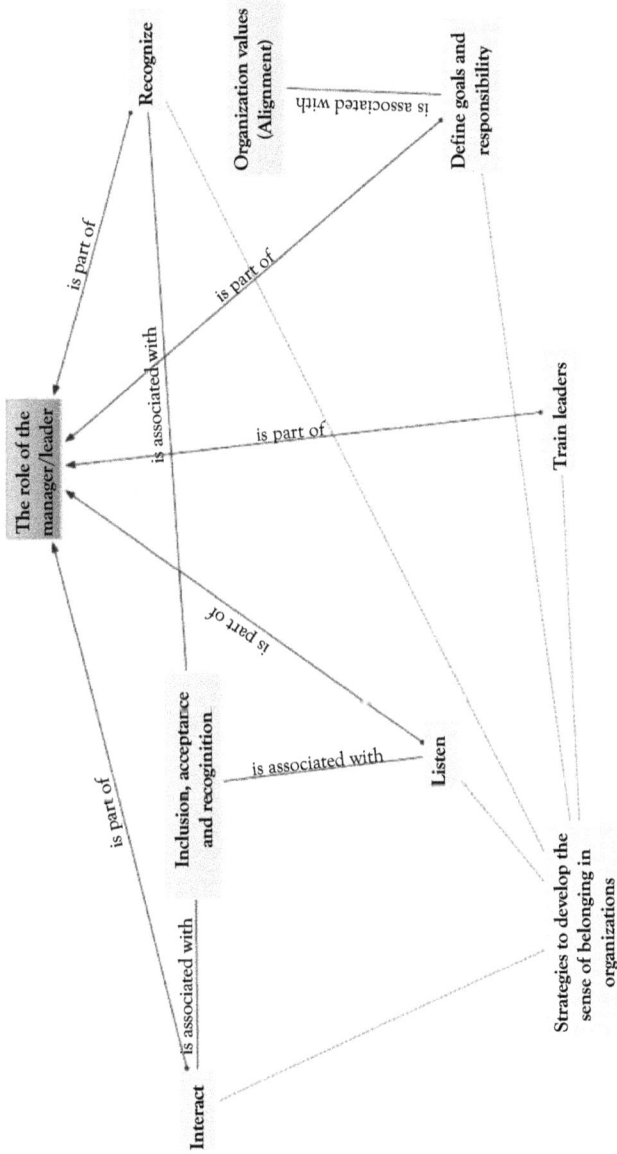

Figure A.7 Strategies to develop the sense of belonging in organizations

Bibliography

2019. *Global Human Capital Trends*. Deloitte Insights.

2020. *Diversity, Equity and Inclusion 4.0. A Toolkit for Leaders to Accelerate Social Progress in the Future of Work*. World Economic Forum.

Aebischer, V., and D. Oberlé. 1998. *Le groupe en psychologie sociale*, 52–53. Paris, Dunod.

Allen, K.A. 2019. "Making Sense of Belonging." *InPsych* 41, no. 3.

Avolio, B.J., W.L. Gardner, F.O. Walumbwa, F. Luthans, and D.R. May. 2004. *Unlocking the Mask: A Look at the Process by Which Authentic Leaders Impact Follower Attitudes and Behaviors*. University of Nebraska Management Department Faculty Publications.

Bass, B.M. 1990. "From Transactional to Transformational Leadership Learning to Share the Vision." *Organizational Dynamics* 18, pp. 19–32.

Batson, C.D. 2009. "These Things Called Empathy." In *The Social Neuroscience of Empathy*, eds. Decety, J., and W. Ickes, Cambridge, MA: MIT Press.

Baumeister, R.F., and M.R. Leary. 1995. "The Need to Belong: Desire for Interpersonal Attachments as a Fundamental Human Motivation." *Psychological Bulletin* 117, no. 3, 497–529, http://dx.doi.org/10.1037/0033-2909.117.3.497

Bennis, W.G., and R.J. Thomas. HBR September 2002 issue. *Crucibles of Leadership*.

BetterUp. 2020. "The Value of Belonging at Work: The Business Case for Investing in Workplace Inclusion." https://betterup.com/en-us/resources/reports/the-value-of-belonging-at-work-the-business-case-for-investing-in-workplace-inclusion

Bion, W.R. 1944. *Experiences in Groups and Other Papers*. Tavistock Publications, 1961

Brown, B. 2017. *Braving the Wilderness: The Quest for True Belonging and the Courage to Stand Alone*. Random House.

Burns, D.D. 1980. *Feeling Good: The New Mood Therapy*. Willian Morrow and Company.

Cacioppo, J. 2013. "The Lethality of Loneliness." *TEDx Talk*, https://youtube.com/watch?v=_0hxl03JoA0

Carr, E.W., R.A. Kellerman, G. Rosen and R. Alexi. 2019. "The Value of Belonging at Work." *The Harvard Business Review*.

Charles, M. March, 2008. "Lingua Franca in Global Business." Paper presented at the ELF Forum: The First International Conference of English as a Lingua Franca, University of Helsinki, Finland.

DeHaas, D.L., B. Bachus, and E. Horn. 2017. *Unleashing the Power of Inclusion.* Deloitte University.

Deloitte. *Uncovering Talent - A New Model of Inclusion.* Deloitte University.

Dixon-Flye, S., K. Dolan, V. Hunt, and S. Prince. 2020. "Diversity Wins: How Inclusion Matters." McKinsey. https://mckinsey.com/featured-insights/diversity-and-inclusion/diversity-wins-how-inclusion-matters?cid=soc-app

Dobbin, F., and A. Kalev. 2016. "Why Diversity Programs Fail." *Harvard Business Review.*

Duhigg, C. 2016. "What Google Learned From Its Quest to Build the Perfect Team." *New York Times,* https://nytimes.com/2016/02/28/magazine/what-google-learned-from-its-quest-to-build-the-perfect-team.html

Edmondson, A. 2019. "Creating Psychological Safety in the Workplace." https://hbr.org/podcast/2019/01/creating-psychological-safety-in-the-workplace

Edmundson, A. December 28, 2018. *Fearless Organizations: Creating Psychological Safety in the Workplace for Learning, Innovation, and Growth.* John Wiley & Sons Inc.

Eisenberger, N.I. 2011. "Why Rejection Hurts: What Social Neuroscience has Revealed About the Brain's Response to Social Rejection." In *Oxford Library of Psychology. The Oxford Handbook of Social Neuroscience,* eds. Decety, J., and Cacioppo, J.T., 586–598. Oxford University Press.

Eisenberger, N.I., and S.W. Cole. 2012. "Social Neuroscience and Health: Neurophysiological Mechanisms Linking Social Ties with Physical Health." *Nature Neuroscience* 15, no. 5, pp. 669–674. PMID: 22504347.

Eisenberger, N.I., M.D. Lieberman, and K.D. Williams. 2003. "Does Rejection Hurt? An fMRI Study of Social Exclusion." *Science* 302, no. 5643, pp. 290–292.

Fredriksson, R., et al. 2006. "The Multinational Corporation as a Multilingual Organization: The Notion of a Common Corporate Language." *Corporate Communications: An International Journal* 11, 406–423. doi: 10.1108/13563280610713879

Gao, W., H. Zhu, K.S. Giovanello, K.J. Smith, J.D. Shen, J.H. Gilmore, and W. Lin. 2009. "Evidence on the Emergence of the Brain's Default Network from 2-Week-Old to 2-Year-Old Healthy Pediatric Subjects." *Proceedings of the National Academy of Sciences* 106, no. 16, 67906795. doi: 10.1073/pnas.0811221106

Goleman, D. 1995. *Emotional Intelligence.* New York, NY: Bantam Books.

Granovetter, M. 1973. "The Strength of Weak Ties." *American Journal of Sociology* 78, no. 6, pp. 1360–1380.

Harris, L. Comment Available at https://theguardian.com/uk-news/2018/dec/02/unconscious-bias-what-is-it-and-can-it-be-eliminated

Jones, G., K.A. Moore, and D. Morgan. 2019. *Leadership: Untapping The Secret to Regional Wellbeing, Belonging and Resilience.* 10.1007/978-981-32-9694-7_8

Junger, S. 2016. *Tribe: On Homecoming and Belonging.* New York, NY: HarperCollins Publishers.

Kachru, B. 1992. "World Englishes: Approaches, Issues and Resources." *Language Teaching* 25, no. 1, 114. doi:10.1017/S0261444800006583

Kahn, W. 2017. "Psychological Conditions of Personal Engagement and Disengagement at Work." *The Academy of Management Journal* 33, no. 4, 692. https://doi.org/10.5465/256287

Kaufman, S.B. April 7, 2020. *Transcend: The New Science of Self-Actualization.*

Knight, R. October, 2014. "How to Get Your Employees to Speak Up." *Harvard Business Review.*

Lazarre, J. 1996. *Beyond the Whiteness of Whiteness: Memoir of a White Mother of Black Sons.* Duke University Press.

Lieberman, M.D. 2013. *Social: Why Our Brains are Wired to Connect.* Tantor Media.

Lorenzo, R., N. Voigt, M. Tsusaka, M, Krentz, and M. Abouzahr. 2018. *How Diverse Leadership Teams Boost Innovation.* Boston Consulting Group.

Mark, S., and M.S. Granovette. 1973. "The Strength of Weak Ties." *American Journal of Sociology* 78, no. 6, pp. 1360–1380.

Maslow, A.H. 1943. "A Theory of Human Motivation." *Psychological Review* 50, no. 4, 370–396. https://doi.org/10.1037/h0054346

Maté, G. 2011. *When the Body Says No: Understanding the Stress-Disease Connection.* Penguin Random House.

Mayer, J.D., P. Salovey, and D.R. Caruso. 2008. "Emotional Intelligence: New Ability or Eclectic Traits?" *Am Psychol* 63, no. 6, 50351/. doi: 10.1037/0003-066X.63.6.503

Mills, J.H., and A.J. Mills. 2009. "Critical Sensemaking and Workplace Inequities." In *Equality, Diversity and Inclusion at Work: A Research Companion*, ed. Ozbilgin, M., 171178. Cheltenham: Edward Elgar Press.

Murthy, V. 2020. *The Healing Power of Human Connection in a Sometimes-Lonely World.* Harper Wave. ISBN: 9780062913296

MyKindaFuture. "The Importance of Belonging in the Workplace." https://mykindafuture.com/2020/06/10/less-than-one-third-of-uk-employees-feel-like-they-belong/

Op-Ed, J.C. "Coronavirus reminds Asian Americans Like Me that Our Belonging is Conditional." https://latimes.com/opinion/story/2020-04-22/asian-american-discrimination-john-cho-coronavirus

Pullin, P. 2010. "Small Talk, Rapport and International Communicative Competence: Lessons to Learn from BELF." *Journal of Business Communication* 47, no. 4, pp. 455–476.

Ramachandran, V.S. 2009. "The Neurons that Shaped Civilization." *TED Talk* https://ted.com/talks/vilayanur_ramachandran_the_neurons_that_shaped_ civilization

Relate. 2014. "The Way We Are Now." Available at https://relate.org.uk/about- us/media-centre/press-releases/2014/8/20/way-we-are-now-new-study- reveals-our-couple-family-friendships-sex-and-work-secrets

Resilience Alliance. 2010. "Assessing Resilience in Social-Ecological Systems: Workbook for Practitioners." Version 2.0. Online: http://resalliance.org/ 3871.php

Rocher, G. 1968. *Introduction à la sociologie générale*. Paris : Ed HMH.

Rogers, C.R. 1980. *A Way of Being*.

Sandstrom, G.M., and E.W. Dunn. 2014. "Is Efficiency Overrated? Minimal Social Interactions Lead to Belonging and Positive Affect." *Social Psychological and Personality Science* 5, pp. 436–441.

Schein, E.H., and A. Schein Peter. 2017. *Organizational Culture and Leadership (The Jossey-Bass Business & Management Series)* 5th ed. Published by John Wiley & Sons Inc.

Schleifer, H. 2010. *The Power of Connection*. TEDx talk in Tel Aviv - https:// youtube.com/watch?v=HEaERAnIqsY

Search Inside Yourself. Program available from Search Inside Yourself Learning Institute. Available at https://siyli.org/programs/search-inside-yourself

Sehmi, S. 2014. "Ten Tips for Effective Communication in English with Non- Natives." Available at https://davidlivermore.com/2014/01/09/10-tips-for- effective-communication-in-english-with-non-natives/

Sehmi, S. 2014. "Ten Tips for Leading a Multicultural Team." *InterNations*. Available at https://internations.org/guide/global/ten-tips-for-leading-a- multicultural-team-17056

Sehmi, S. 2014. "Ten tips on Being an Effective Global Leader." *InterNations*. Available at https://internations.org/guide/global/ten-tips-on-being-an- effective-global-leader-17460

Sehmi, S. 2020. *Thrive Global January 1, 2020 The Five Invitations: Discovering what Death Can Teach us About Living Fully*.

Snyder-Mackler, et al. 2020. "Social Determinants of Health and Survival in Humans and Other Animals." *Science* 368, no. 843.

The EY Belonging Barometer. 2019. Available at https://ey.com/en_us/diversity- inclusiveness/ey-belonging-barometer-workplace-study

Todorov, A. 2017. *Face Value: The Irresistible Influence of First Impressions*. Princeton University Press.

Turner, J.C. 1975. "Social Comparison and Social Identity: Some Prospects for Intergroup Behavior." *European Journal of Social Psychology* 5, pp. 5–34.

Van Hoof, E. 2020. "This is the Psychological Side of the COVID-19 Pandemic that We're Ignoring." *World Economic Forum.* https://weforum.org/agenda/2020/ 04/this-is-the-psychological-side-of-the-covid-19-pandemic-that-were-ignoring/

Van Orden, K.A., T.K. Witte, K.C. Cukrowicz, S.R. Braithwaite, E.A. Selby, and T.E. Joiner, Jr. 2010. "The Interpersonal Theory of Suicide." *Psychological Review* 117, no. 2, 575600. doi:10.1037 /a0018697

Volini, E, J. Schwartz, and I. Roy. 2019. *Organizational Performance: It's a Team Sport.*

Wakefield, J.R.H., et al. 2017. "The Relationship Between Group Identification and Satisfaction with Life in a Cross-Cultural Community Sample." *Journal of Happiness Studies* 18, pp. 785–807.

Xu X, X. Zuo, X, Wang, and S. Han. 2009. "Do you Feel My Pain? Racial Group Membership Modulates Empathic Neural Responses." *Journal of Personality and Social Psychology* 29, no. 26, 8525–8529. doi:10.1523/ JNEUROSCI.2418-09.2009

Bibliography for Research—Technical

Achterberg, P., D. Houtman, S. Aupers, W. Koster, P. Mascini, and J. Waal. 2009. "Christian Cancellation of the Secularist Truce? Waning Christian Religiosity and Waxing Religious Derivatization in the West." *In Journal for the Scientific Study of Religion* 48, pp. 687–701.

Aebischer, V., and D. Oberlé. 1998. *Le Groupe En Psychologie Sociale.* Paris. Dunod.

Allen, K., M.L. Kern, D. Vella-Brodrick, J. Hattie, and L. Waters. 2018. "What Schools Need to Know about Fostering School Belonging: A Meta-Analysis." *Educ Psychol Rev* 30, no. 1, pp. 1–34.

Arain, M., M. Haque, L. Johal, P. Mathur, W. Nel, A. Rais, and S. Sharma. 2013. "Maturation of the Adolescent Brain." *Neuropsychiatric Disease and Treatment* 9, pp. 449–461.

Aron, A., E. Melinat, E.N. Aron, R.D. Vallone, and R.J. Bator. 1997. "The Experimental Generation of Interpersonal Closeness: A Procedure and Some Preliminary Findings." *Personality and Social Psychology Bulletin* 23, no. 4, pp. 363–377.

Baumeister, R.F., and M.R. Leary. 1995. "The Need to Belong: Desire for Interpersonal Attachments as a Fundamental Human Motivation." *Psychological Bulletin* 117, no. 3, 497–529. https://doi.org/10.1037/0033-2909.117.3.497

Bennett, M.J. 2004. *Becoming Interculturally Competent., Toward Multi-culturalism: A Reader in Multicultural Education.* ed. J.S. Wurzel. Newton, MA: Intercultural Resource.

Billis, D., ed. 2020. "Handbook on Hybrid Organizations." Emeritus Reader, London School of Economics and Colin Rochester, Honorary Research Fellow, University of Kent, UK. In, 576 . Edward Elgar Publishing.

Blakemore, S.J. 2008. "The Social Brain in Adolescence." *Nature Reviews Neuroscience* 9, no. 4, pp. 267–77.

Braddock, J.H., and A.D.C. Gonzalez. 2010. "Social Isolation and Social Cohesion: The Effects of K-12 Neighborhood and School Segregation on Intergroup Orientations." *Teachers College Record* 112, no. 6, pp. 1631–1653.

Brown, H.D. n.d. *Principles of Language Learning and Teaching.* Englewood Cliffs: Prentice Hall Regents.

Burnett, S., C. Sebastian, K.C. Kadosh, and S.J. Blakemore. 2011. "The Social Brain in Adolescence: Evidence from Functional Magnetic Resonance Imaging and Behavioral Studies." *Neuroscience & Biobehavioral Reviews* 35, no. 8, pp. 1654–1664.

Casanova, J. 1994. *Public Religions in the Modern World.* Chicago, London: University of Chicago Press.

Castilla, E.J., and S. Benard. 2010. "The Paradox of Meritocracy in Organizations." *Administrative Science Quarterly* 55, no. 4, pp. 543–676.

Devers, C.J., D. Daugherty, T. Steenbergh, J. Runyan, L. Oke, A. Alayan, and E. Ragsdale. 2016. *"Mindsets, Smartphones, and Student Success."* In Proceedings of World Conference on E-Learning in Corporate, Government, Healthcare, and Higher Education 2016, 576–579. Chesapeake, VA: AACE.

DeWall, C.N., G. MacDonald, G.D. Webster, C.L. Masten, R.F. Baumeister, C. Powell, and N.I. Eisenberger. 2010. "Acetaminophen Reduces Social Pain: Behavioral and Neural Evidence." *Psychological Science* 21, no. 7, 931. https://doi.org/10.1177/0956797610374741

Dweck, C.S.M. 2006. *The New Psychology of Success.* New York, NY: Ballantine Books.

Edmondson, A.C. 2011. *"Strategies for Learning from Failure."* Harvard Business Review.

Eisenberger, N.I., M.D. Lieberman, and K.D. Williams. 2003. "Does Rejection Hurt? An fMRI Study of Social Exclusion." *Science* 302, no. 5643, pp. 290–292.

Eisenberger, N.I., and S.W. Cole. 2012. "Social Neuroscience and Health: Neurophysiological Mechanisms Linking Social Ties with Physical Health." *Nature Neuroscience* 15, no. 5, pp. 669–674.

Everett, M.R., B.H. William, and M. Yoshitaka. 2002. "Edward T. Hall and The History of Intercultural Communication: The United States and Japan." *Keio.*

Fowler, S.M./ M., and M.G. 1995.

Gao, W.Z., G. H., K. S., K.J. Smith, J.D. Shen, J.H. Gilmore, and W. Lin. 2009. "Evidence on the Emergence of the Brain's Default Network from 2-Week-Old to 2-Year-Old Healthy Pediatric Subjects." *Proceedings of the National Academy of Sciences* 106, no. 16, pp. 6790–95. https://doi.org/10.1073/pnas.0811221106.

Harrist, A.W., and K.D. Bradley. 2002. "Social Exclusion in the Classroom: Teachers and Students as Agents of Change." In Improving Academic Achievement, ed. J. Aronson, 363–83. New York, NY: Academic Press.

Hofstede, G. January 2005. *Cultures and Organizations: Software of the Mind.* Revised and Expanded 2nd. New York.

Hofstede, G. 2001. *Cultural Consequences*, 2nd ed. SAGE Publishing.

Katzenbach, J.R., and D.K. Smith. 1999. The Wisdom of Teams.

Knight, R. 2017. "7 Practical Ways to Reduce Bias in Your Hiring Process." *Harvard Business Review.*

Langille, D.B., M. Asbridge, A. Cragg, and D. Rasic. 2015. "Associations of School Connectedness with Adolescent Suicidality: Gender Differences and the Role of Risk of Depression." *The Canadian Journal of Psychiatry* 60, no. 6, pp. 258–267.

Leslie, S.J., A. Cimpian, M. Meyer, and E. Freeland. 2015. "Expectations of Brilliance Underlie Gender Distributions across Academic Disciplines." *Science* 347, no. 6219, pp. 262–265.

Marraccini, M.E., and Z.M. Brier. 2017. "School Connectedness and Suicidal Thoughts and Behaviors: A Systematic Meta-Analysis." *School Psychology Quarterly* 32, no. 1, p. 5.

Matthews, T., A. Danese, J. Wertz, A. Ambler, M. Kelly, A. Diver, and L. Arseneault. 2015. "Social Isolation and Mental Health at Primary and Secondary School Entry: A Longitudinal Cohort Study." *Journal of the American Academy of Child & Adolescent Psychiatry* 54, no. 3, pp. 225–232.

Mucchielli, A. 1986. *Léidentité.* Paris: PUF.

Nater, C., and S. Sczesny. 2016. "Affirmative Action Policies in Job Advertisements for Leadership Positions: How They Affect Women's and Men's Inclination to Apply." *European Journal of Social Psychology* 46, no. 7, pp. 891–902.

O.E.C.D. 2017. PISA 2015 Results (Volume III): Students' Well-Being. Paris: OECD Publishing. https://doi.org/10.1787/9789264273856-11-en.

"Op-Ed: John Cho: Coronavirus Reminds Asian Americans like Me That Our Belonging Is Conditional." n.d. https://latimes.com/opinion/story/2020-04-22/asian-american-discrimination-john-cho-coronavirus

Rogers, C.R. 1951. *Client-Centered Therapy.* Oxford, England: Houghton Mifflin.

Schneider Susan, C., and B. Jean-Louis. 2003. *Managing Across Cultures, 2nd.* ed.

Sloane, P. 2012. *The Leader's Guide to Lateral Thinking Skills Unlocking the Creativity and Innovation in You and Your Team.* London: Kogan Page.

Snyder, K. 2014. "The Abrasiveness Trap: High-Achieving Men and Women Are Described Differently in Reviews." *Fortune Magazine*, pp. 627–660.

Sobel, D. 2017. *The Glass Universe : How the Ladies of the Harvard Observatory Took the Measure of the Stars.* New York, NY: Penguin Books.

Sperber, D. 1996. Explaining Culture Culturalistic Approach Blackwell Publishing.

Stallen, M., C.K. De Dreu, S. Shalvi, A. Smidts, and A.G. Sanfey. 2012. "The Herding Hormone: Oxytocin Stimulates in-Group Conformity." *Psychological Science* 23, no. 11, pp. 1288–1292.

Steele, C.M. 2010. *Whistling Vivaldi: and Other Clues to How Stereotypes Affect Us.* New York, NY: W.W. Norton & Co.

Swaby, R. 2015. *Headstrong: 52 Women Who Changed Science – and the World.* New York, NY: Broadway Books.

Symposium Proceedings. 2002. *An Interim Step toward a Conceptual Framework for the Practice of Diversity.* Waltham,. MA: Bentley College.

Ting-Toomey, S., and J.G. Oetzel. 2001. *Managing Intercultural Conflict Effectively.* London: Sage Publications.

Trompenaars, F. 1997. *Riding The Waves of Culture: Understanding Belonging in Global Business with Charles Hampden-Turner.*

Trompenaars, F. 2000. *Building Cross-Cultural Competence: How to Create Wealth from Conflicting Values With.* Charles Hampden-Turner and David Lewis.

Turner, J.C. 1979. 'Comparaison sociale et identité sociale: quelques perspectives pour l'étude du comportement intergroupes.' *Experiences entre groupes*, 151–184. In , ed. W. Doise, 154. Paris: Mouton.

Why Diverse Teams Are Smarter David Rock and Heidi Grant HBR November 04, 2016

Wike, T.L., and M.W. Fraser. 2009. "School Shootings: Making Sense of the Senseless." *Aggression and Violent Behavior* 14, no. 3, 162–169. doi: 10.1016/j.avb.2009.01.005

Articles used from My Client Resources:

2018 Campaign against casual sexism at UN Geneva - UNOG, May 2018

Accelerating gender equality - CERN Courier, April 2017

ASSET 2016: experiences surrounding gender equality in STEMM academia and the intersections with ethnicity, sexual orientation, disability and age - ECU.

Avoid unconscious bias in letters of recommendation - NCWIT, 2010

Barthelemy, R.S., M. McCormick, and C. Henderson. 2016. "Gender Discrimination in Physics and Astronomy: Graduate Student Experiences of Sexism and Gender Microaggressions." *Physical Review Physics Education Research* 12, no. 2, p. 020119.

CERN offers UN advice on bringing more women into science - Symmetry, March 2013

Competent Men and Warm Women: Gender Stereotypes and Backlash in Image Search Results - Open University of Cyprus, University of Sheffield, UK, 2017

EPRRTC - a research project to identify and improve the situation of employees with disability- Cornell University, 2014

Être LGBT au travail: Résultats d'une recherche en Suisse (FR) - UNIGE, October 2015

EY explores belonging in the workplace, with new Belonging Barometer study New York, 1 Nov 2018

Fabiola Gianotti to speak at UN on violence against women - CERN Updates, March 2014

Femmes et pouvoir: le grand tabou (FR) – Huffington Post, September 2013

Gendered Innovations: How Gender Analysis Contributes to Research - European Commission, July 2013

Happy Men - Solidarity initiative for professional gender equality (FR) - August 2015

Implicit bias in academia: A challenge to the meritocratic principle and to women's careers – And what to do about it - LERU group, January 2018

Op-ed: Good men should not be quiet spectators: Is shared outcry bringing an end to the cruel privilege of impunity? - UN Women, October 2017

She Figures 2015 - European Commission, Directorate General for Research and Innovation, 2016

Stephen Hawking presents the Intel connected wheelchair - Tech Times, September 2014

Studies related to gender and geographic diversity in the ATLAS Collaboration - ATLAS Collaboration, July 2016

That's what zhe said: mx-ing up the language of gender - The Conversation, January 2016

US kids' doodles of scientists reveal changing stereotypes - Nature, March 2018

Why Are There Still So Few Women in Science? - The New York Times, October 2013

Women are less likely to study STEM subjects – but disadvantaged women are even less so - UCL Institute of Education, IOE London Blog, 2017

About the Author

Sunita Sehmi is the founder of Walk the Talk, where she provides coaching and diversity and inclusion (D&I) consulting services to global companies and nongovernmental organizations (NGOs). Her clients include the CERN, GAVI Alliance, Facebook, IMD Business School, The Tata Group, McKinsey, and Novartis, to name but a few.

She supports CxOs, senior executives, and their teams to enhance their effectiveness, enabling them to foster exceptional leadership and collaborative behaviors.

Sunita brings over 25 years' experience and knowledge and has a rich and diverse background, (she is Indian, British, and Swiss). Through her work, Sunita aims to reinforce belonging within organizations, leading to more inclusive groups and teams.

Sunita studied Organizational and Developmental Psychology at bachelor level and the Development and Training of Adults at postgraduate level in the United Kingdom. Moreover, she holds a master's degree in Coaching and Career Management from the University of Geneva School of Economics and Management. She is an ICF-accredited Executive Coach, NLP Practitioner, and has certification from INSEAD in Gender Diversity.

In her free time, Sunita is a pro-bono mentor for the Richard Branson Center of Entrepreneurship and a volunteer at the Hospice La Maison De Tara. An avid writer, Sunita is a content writer at Forbes Middle East and Thrive Global. *The Power of Belonging* is Sunita's second book; her first book is titled *How to Get Out of Your Own Way, For Women Who Want to Win.*

On a more personal level, of Indian origin and brought up in London, Sunita lives in Geneva with her husband and two adult sons. She enjoys spending time with them and entertaining her many friends from round the world. She highly values her Indian heritage, particularly when it comes to cooking.

Index

OTHER TITLES IN THE BUSINESS CAREER DEVELOPMENT COLLECTION

Vilma Barr, Consultant, Editor

- *The Trust Factor* by Russell von Frank
- *Financing New Ventures* by Geoffrey Gregson
- *Strategic Bootstrapping* by Matthew W. Rutherford
- *Creating A Business and Personal Legacy* by Mark J. Munoz
- *Innovative Selling* by Eden White
- *Present! Connect!* by Tom Guggino
- *Introduction to Business* by Patrice Flynn
- *Be Different!* by Stan Silverman

Concise and Applied Business Books

The Collection listed above is one of 30 business subject collections that Business Expert Press has grown to make BEP a premiere publisher of print and digital books. Our concise and applied books are for...

- Professionals and Practitioners
- Faculty who adopt our books for courses
- Librarians who know that BEP's Digital Libraries are a unique way to offer students ebooks to download, not restricted with any digital rights management
- Executive Training Course Leaders
- Business Seminar Organizers

Business Expert Press books are for anyone who needs to dig deeper on business ideas, goals, and solutions to everyday problems. Whether one print book, one ebook, or buying a digital library of 110 ebooks, we remain the affordable and smart way to be business smart. For more information, please visit www.businessexpertpress.com, or contact sales@businessexpertpress.com.